Roaming Retreat: RV Camping Bliss in America's National Treasures

Journeying through Nature's Wonders on Wheels

Dylan Hart

Table of Contents

INTRODUCTION

Welcome to "Roaming Retreat: RV Camping Bliss in America's National Treasures," where the call of the open road and the wonders of nature converge to create an unforgettable journey on wheels. In this e-book, we invite you to embark on a unique adventure through the heart of America's most spectacular landscapes, experiencing the joy of RV camping amidst the nation's cherished national treasures.

The allure of the open road has always held a special place in the hearts of adventurers, and RV camping offers a front-row seat to the beauty that defines the United States. Whether you are a seasoned RV enthusiast or a novice eager to explore, this guide will serve as your companion, providing insights, tips, and inspiration for an enriching and immersive travel experience.

As we journey through the chapters of this e-book, you will discover the art of planning the perfect RV adventure, from selecting the ideal rig for your needs to crafting an itinerary that explores both iconic national parks and hidden gems off the beaten path. We delve into the nuances of setting up camp, creating a comfortable outdoor living space, and connecting with the natural wonders that await just beyond your RV door.

Beyond the practicalities of RV travel, "Roaming Retreat" celebrates the community and camaraderie that blossoms among fellow road warriors. From sharing stories around the campfire to joining RV clubs and events, the journey becomes as much about the people you meet as the places you explore.

Whether you seek the thrill of hiking through untouched wilderness, savoring local flavors on the road, or simply finding solace in the quietude of nature, this e-book is your guide to maximizing the RV experience. Join us as we navigate the challenges, celebrate the triumphs, and embrace the transformative power of RV camping in America's national treasures. The road beckons, and the adventure awaits – let the Roaming Retreat begin!

CHAPTER I

The Call of the Open Road

Exploring the Allure of RV Travel

Exploring the allure of RV travel unveils a world of freedom, flexibility, and adventure that captivates the hearts of both seasoned road warriors and newcomers to the open road. In its most fundamental form, recreational vehicle travel departs from traditional vacations. It provides a one-of-a-kind combination of ease of use, comfort, and a profound connection with the natural world. Traveling in this manner is not merely a means of transportation; instead, it is a way of life that encourages individuals to break free from routine constraints and embark on a voyage of self-discovery.

RV travel is a popular option because it liberates

travelers from the constraints of traditional vacations. It offers an unmatched level of flexibility, allowing individuals to chart their own course, free from the confines of hotel bookings and predetermined itineraries. This freedom to choose when to go, where to halt, and how long to dwell in each destination transforms the wide road into a canvas for their journeys. This autonomy generates a sense of spontaneity and release, enabling travelers to embrace the unknown and appreciate the fortuitous discoveries that frequently define the RV experience.

Traveling in a recreational vehicle (RV) appeals to the

common desire for a secure and familiar environment, even on the road. The RV can be transformed into a pleasant refuge, furnished with all the comforts and conveniences of home. Despite the ever-changing landscapes, this mobile home becomes a haven, providing a comfortable and familiar location. The appeal of having one's lodging on wheels is not just about luxury; it's about the release from the logistical constraints of typical travel, fostering a sense of security and self-sufficiency that resonates with every adventurer.

Because RV travelers are not restricted to the typical tourist sites, the journey itself becomes an essential component of the destination where they are traveling. The ability to travel off the beaten road, uncover hidden jewels in the country, and explore distant regions of the country that are inaccessible to more extensive modes of transit makes this mode of transportation so appealing. Because of its elegant and versatile character, the recreational vehicle (RV) provides access to isolated campgrounds, stunning panoramas, and natural treasures that still need to be explored. This close relationship with the landscapes helps to cultivate a profound appreciation for the variety and beauty that characterize the physical landscape of the United States.

The allure of traveling in a recreational vehicle lies in its practical benefits and the profound connection with nature it facilitates. Unlike air or conventional road trips, RV journeys allow travelers to immerse themselves in the natural environment when they leave their mobile homes. The rhythmic hum of the road, the aroma of pine forests, and the crisp mountain air become constant companions. RV travelers often wake up to the soft rustle of leaves or fall asleep under a canvas of stars, fostering a deep connection with the natural world that is unmatched by any other style of travel.

This connection with nature extends beyond the immediate settings in which it is experienced. Traveling in a recreational vehicle (RV) frequently involves visiting national parks and other natural wonders, encouraging individuals to investigate the various ecosystems comprising the American landscape. RV travelers can view the unique beauty of these national treasures up close and personal. These national treasures range from the Rocky Mountains' towering peaks to the Grand Canyon's vast expanse or wherever in between. The fascination originates from the visual spectacle and the opportunity to interact with the environment actively. This can be accomplished through activities such as hiking, observing wildlife, or simply enjoying nature's peace and quiet.

To add insult to injury, the attractiveness of traveling in a recreational vehicle is intricately connected to the sense of community that develops when traveling. RV enthusiasts get together to build a warm and inclusive community, and a shared passion unites them for traveling and experiencing new things. Campgrounds transform into social hubs where people gather to share their experiences through the sharing of stories, forming friendships, and developing a sense of camaraderie. A recreational vehicle (RV) lifestyle enables a more extended and meaningful connection with persons with the same passion for the open road, in contrast to regular vacations, which may only involve brief interactions with other tourists.

Exploring the fascination of traveling in a recreational vehicle (RV) is an invitation to embrace a way of life beyond the typical lifestyle. This encourages people to rethink their connection with travel by placing more importance on their experiences than the places they visit and the journey itself rather than the destination itself. The recreational vehicle transforms into more than just a vehicle; it becomes a gateway to a world of boundless opportunities, where the road becomes a medium through which one may find oneself, experience new things, and make memories that will last a lifetime. The charm of RV travel continues to shine brightly, enticing all those with a sense of adventure to join the caravan and go on a journey unlike any other. This is because more people seek a break from the commonplace and a reunion with the essence of discovery.

Benefits of Choosing RV Camping

The decision to camp in a recreational vehicle (RV) as a mode of transportation and lodging reveals many advantages that respond to the aspirations of contemporary adventurers looking for an unparalleled and freeing experience. The unrivaled sensation of independence that RV camping provides is at the heart of the attractiveness of this outdoor activity. In contrast to those who take traditional holidays, which frequently include predetermined timetables and reservations, RV campers find themselves free from the constraints of rigorous work schedules. This independence extends beyond the limitations of established arrangements, enabling passengers to chart their course, make impromptu course corrections, and enjoy the journey just as much as they want the destination itself.

A further advantage of RV camping is that it allows

people to break free from the confines of traditional lodgings and establish a relationship with the space in which they live. More than merely a means of mobility, the recreational vehicle (RV) evolves into a mobile house that can be moved around. While surrounded by the ever-changing beauty of the open road, this mobility provides the conveniences of home, such as a well-equipped kitchen and a cozy sleeping space. The capability of transporting one's dwelling wherever the adventure may take one develops a sense of familiarity and security, transforming the recreational vehicle into a customized sanctuary amidst the vast landscapes of the great outdoors on the journey.

Not only is camping in a recreational vehicle (RV) a cost-

effective alternative to traditional vacations, but it also provides personal freedom and comfort. While the initial investment in an RV may seem substantial, the long-term benefits become evident as travelers reduce their expenses on accommodation and food. The self-sufficient nature of the RV allows people to cook their meals, eliminating the need for costly restaurant dining. Campgrounds, often more affordable than hotels, offer services from electricity hookups to communal facilities, further enhancing the economic appeal of RV camping. This facet of RV travel makes it an accessible choice for a diverse range of enthusiasts, from retirees exploring the world on a fixed income to families seeking a memorable holiday.

Additionally, compared to other modes of transportation, the influence of RV camping on the environment is significantly less significant. In addition to being built to be more fuel-efficient than bigger cars, recreational vehicles (RVs) can also cook meals within the RV, which reduces the need for throwaway containers and utensils. In addition, campgrounds are increasingly embracing environmentally friendly methods, which encourage responsible trash disposal and the conservation of resources. Campers who use recreational vehicles frequently find that they are associating themselves with a sustainable and conscious approach to travel. This allows them to lessen their environmental impact and leave behind a lower carbon footprint than those who engage in more traditional types of tourism.

A stronger connection with nature is fostered by RV camping, which encourages a more immersive and genuine vacation experience. This is in addition to the practical advantages that RV camping offers. While exploring areas that are typically inaccessible to traditional tourists, RV enthusiasts find that the journey becomes an essential component of the adventure. Campsites tucked away in the middle of nature become temporary homes for tourists. They are places where they can wake up to the sound of leaves rustling and fall asleep under a blanket of stars. A sense of quiet and rejuvenation is increasingly sought in today's fast-paced world. This intimate contact with the natural world contrasts the sterile environment of hotels and resorts, delivering a sense of peace and relaxation that is in high demand.

In addition, camping in a recreational vehicle gives you access to various locations, ranging from popular national parks to peaceful lakeside areas. The mobility of the recreational vehicle enables guests to see well-known landmarks and lesser-known treasures off the main path. It is possible to have a direct and immediate relationship with the landscapes that characterize the beauty of the voyage by camping in an RV. This can be accomplished by experiencing the dawn over the Grand Canyon or by camping next to a lake in the mountains that is clear and unspoiled. Individuals can cultivate a sense of wonder and respect for the unique fabric of the American terrain by selecting campgrounds tucked in the heart of nature. This allows individuals to wake up to genuinely breathtaking panoramic views.

Camping in a recreational vehicle (RV) is especially appealing to people looking for a sense of community and companionship while traveling. Campgrounds are transformed into social hubs where people with similar interests converse about their experiences, offer advice, and revel in the excitement of adventuring over the campfire. RV camping, in contrast to the more isolated experiences typically associated with traditional travel, fosters the development of friendships, hence fostering the formation of a tight-knit community bonded together by a shared passion for the open road. This sense of connection continues beyond the confines of the campsite, as RV clubs and events offer extra opportunities for enthusiasts to get together and enjoy the passion they share.

In conclusion, the advantages of camping in an RV go much beyond the conventional travel considerations typically associated with it. The modern yearning for independence, flexibility, and a more profound connection with the world that surrounds us is captured by this lifestyle option, which resonates with the modern-day desire. Individuals can break away from the restraints of routine and enjoy the spontaneity of the open road when they go RV camping because it provides a unique blend of comfort and excitement. RV camping corresponds with the values of an increasing number of visitors looking for a more personalized, sustainable, and rewarding approach to discovering the wonders of the globe. RV camping offers several other benefits, including economic advantages and environmental concerns. It is a monument to the everlasting spirit of exploration that characterizes the essence of travel, and the appeal of RV camping continues to capture the imaginations of adventurers on a significant scale.

Overcoming Common Misconceptions

For prospective travelers to fully appreciate the freeing and enriching experience that awaits them on the open road, they need to overcome common misconceptions regarding RV camping. There needs to be more understanding that RV travel is reserved solely for people who are retired or who are interested in leading a nomadic lifestyle. The world of recreational vehicle camping is, in fact, extremely diversified since it caters to individuals of all ages, including families, young adventurers, and individuals of all ages. The fact that there is a wide range of recreational vehicles (RV) available, ranging from small trailers to luxurious motorhomes, guarantees that there is a suitable option for any lifestyle and preference. This disproves the concept that RV camping is restricted to a particular population.

Another common misunderstanding that discourages

people who would otherwise be interested in recreational vehicles is the notion that this mode of transportation is unreasonably expensive. Although the initial investment in a recreational vehicle (RV) can be costly, it is essential to see it as a long-term investment that can generate significant savings over time. By providing self-contained living space and kitchen facilities, RV camping enables tourists to reduce the amount of money they spend on expenses related to lodging and food. This contrasts traditional vacations, which typically require frequent hotel stays and dining out. This makes RV travel an accessible choice for people with a wide variety of budgets because campgrounds are inexpensive, which is another factor contributing to RV travel's cost-effectiveness.

One of the most widespread misconceptions about RV camping is that it takes a high level of mechanical expertise or driving competency. The fact is that most people, regardless of their level of competence regarding automobiles, can operate a recreational vehicle (RV). Manufacturers design recreational vehicles (RVs) to have features that are easy to use, and many of them come with contemporary comforts like automatic gearboxes, power steering, and backup cameras, which make driving easier. Those individuals who still need to prepare to commit to purchasing a recreational vehicle (RV) can also take advantage of rental options, which allow them to test the waters and overcome any initial concerns they may have.

As soon as you step inside a contemporary recreational vehicle (RV), you will quickly dispel the myth that camping in an RV is linked with compromising comfort. These cars are outfitted with amenities comparable to those found in conventional residences. These amenities include fully working kitchens, huge bathrooms, and comfortable sleeping quarters. Incorporating entertainment systems, climate control, and other luxuries that enhance the camping experience has been made possible by technological advancements brought about by the advent of new technologies. It is a common misconception that camping requires one to endure discomfort; nevertheless, RV campers enjoy the ease and comfort of a home on wheels, which challenges the notion that camping requires an individual to take the pain.

It is a common misconception that RV camping is a solitary and isolated activity. This is another fallacy surrounding RV camping. Despite appearances, RV campgrounds are thriving communities that unite people with similar interests and experiences to form friendships and share stories. These common areas promote a sense of camaraderie that is frequently lacking in more traditional modes of travel. This sense of camaraderie can be fostered through structured activities and impromptu gatherings around the campfire. The experience of camping in a recreational vehicle (RV) is not isolated; instead, it offers a wealth of opportunities for social contact and the development of long-lasting connections.

It is also a common misunderstanding that RV travel is restricted to particular times of the year or climates. Camping in a recreational vehicle (RV) is a year-round pastime that offers a variety of possibilities for each season, even though certain places are subject to severe weather conditions. Many recreational vehicles (RVs) are outfitted with heating and cooling systems, enabling them to be utilized for both summer and winter vacations. The notion that recreational vehicle travel is limited to certain seasons of the year is debunked by the fact that RV enthusiasts can easily explore a variety of landscapes regardless of the weather, provided they appropriately prepare themselves and have the appropriate equipment.

The maintenance and care of a recreational vehicle (RV) can be a source of concern for prospective travelers, which may discourage them from exploring this means of adventure. On the other hand, contemporary recreational vehicles are built with longevity and ease of maintenance in mind. The chance of mechanical problems can be considerably reduced by performing routine maintenance, conducting frequent inspections, and following the guidelines provided by the manufacturer. In addition, the availability of mobile repair services and the expansion of the network of RV service providers have made it simpler for RV owners to address their maintenance needs in a timely manner, guaranteeing a hassle-free and enjoyable vacation experience.

One of the most common misunderstandings about RV camping is that it is restricted to authorized campgrounds, which limits the opportunity to explore off-grid or remote regions. In addition to the conveniences that campsites provide, such as hookups for water and electricity, RV travelers can also boondocking or dry camping in more remote places. The capability for off-grid camping has increased thanks to technological advancements such as solar panels and efficient battery systems. This has made it possible for RV enthusiasts to enjoy nature's peace and quiet without giving up the luxuries of modern life. This disproves the conventional wisdom that camping in a recreational vehicle (RV) is limited to crowded campgrounds, demonstrating the adaptability and diversity of this form of transportation.

Some people are under the impression that traveling in an RV is harmful to the environment. Even though recreational vehicles (RVs) utilize fuel, modern RVs have become more ecologically friendly due to improvements in engine efficiency and the utilization of alternative fuel solutions. In addition, the promotion of environmentally responsible conduct among RV enthusiasts is facilitated by the focus placed on responsible camping practices, such as Leave No Trace principles. The concept that recreational vehicle travel and environmental conservation may coexist harmonically is further supported by the selection of campgrounds emphasizing sustainability and efforts to minimize the impact on natural surroundings.

For individuals to truly appreciate the vast and enriching world that awaits them on the open road, they need to overcome the prevalent misunderstandings that are associated with RV camping. Understanding the truth of RV travel opens the door to a transforming and liberating experience. This is because it challenges preconceived beliefs about the cost, comfort, and environmental effects of RV travel and dispels stereotypes about the demographics of RV enthusiasts. In the process of breaking free from preconceived beliefs and embracing the adaptability of RV camping, an increasing number of individuals are discovering a lifestyle that provides them with freedom, community, and a profound connection with the world's natural wonders. The path leading to the end of these preconceptions provides the way for a journey that goes beyond expectations and extends an invitation to anyone looking for an adventure to investigate the countless possibilities that RV camping offers.

CHAPTER II

Planning Your RV Adventure

Selecting the Right RV for Your Journey

Making the ideal RV for your trip is crucial to setting the stage for a relaxing and delightful travel experience. Adventurers with different tastes, demands, and travel methods are catered to by the wide variety of recreational vehicles on the market. One of the most critical factors is the kind of RV that best suits your vacation goals. Each type of recreational vehicle— motorhome, travel trailer, fifth wheel, and pop-up camper—offers unique features and benefits. Motorhomes (classes A, B, and C) have a fully integrated experience with a built-in living area. At the same time, fifth wheels and travel trailers allow you to explore your location without pulling all the living quarters. Conversely, pop-up campers offer a lightweight and portable choice for individuals looking for portability and ease of use.

In addition to RV type, size is a crucial consideration while making a choice. The living area, mobility, and accessibility of an RV are all impacted by its size. Larger RVs have more roomy interiors and amenities, but parking and maneuvering through congested areas may require more work. On the other hand, smaller RVs may have less living space but are more maneuverable. Selecting the right size for your RV requires careful consideration of your travel preferences, comfort level, and the places you want to visit.

Understanding your spending limit and other financial factors is crucial to choosing the ideal RV. RVs are available at various prices, from affordable choices to opulent ones with premium features. It's critical to account for recurring costs like maintenance, fuel, campground fees, and possible financing in addition to the original purchase price. In addition to reducing your alternatives, creating a realistic budget guarantees that your RV trip fits your financial objectives.

It is crucial to consider the floor layout when considering buying an RV. The living area's arrangement significantly impacts how practical and comfortable your travels are. Whether you value having a vast bathroom, a separate bedroom, or a large kitchen, looking at the floor plan makes it easier for you to picture your daily life in the RV. Aspects like how you want to sleep, how you want to sit, and how the living area flows should all account for your tastes and the needs of your traveling companions.

Evaluating the features and facilities that come with the RV is equally significant. Modern recreational vehicles have many amenities, including fully functional kitchens and bathrooms, entertainment systems, and climate control. Sort characteristics according to importance and how long you plan to go. Features like lots of storage, a dependable heating and cooling system, and a cozy sleeping place become essential for anyone thinking about long-term travel or living there permanently. On the other hand, weekend travelers might concentrate on amenities that improve the trip experience without needing much living space.

If you decide to go with a towable RV, like a travel trailer or fifth wheel, you must consider your car's weight and towing capabilities. Comprehending the towing capacity of your car guarantees a secure and compelling journey. Manufacturers list their vehicles' towing capacity, so choosing an RV that complies with these guidelines is critical. A seamless and safe towing experience is also facilitated by purchasing the proper towing equipment and ensuring your car can support the weight.

The decision between new and used RVs brings another complexity to the process. New RVs are expensive but include the latest features, warranties, and technology. However, used RVs could offer a more affordable choice, allowing you to buy a higher-end model for less. When choosing a used RV, it is essential to do a comprehensive check and learn about the vehicle's maintenance history. Depreciation, resale value, and general RV condition are some factors that affect the choice between new and used.

An essential part of the selection process is considering your intended use of the RV. Are you considering moving full-time, taking long road journeys, or going on weekend travels? RVs come in a variety of varieties to suit different kinds of uses. Long-term travelers or people who intend to live in their RVs may choose more significant, more fully furnished versions, but smaller, more mobile RVs may be plenty for quick getaways. Knowing what you want to use your RV for will help you choose one that fits your lifestyle and has the features you need to achieve your travel objectives.

An RV's dependability and performance can be significantly inferred from its maker and model's reputation and reviews. You may assess RV owners' reliability, quality, and general satisfaction with a specific brand or model by looking up consumer reviews, industry ratings, and professional comments. Pay attention to typical problems that owners have reported; this information will help you make an informed selection and choose an RV with a track record of dependability.

A practical factor that's sometimes missed in the enthusiasm for the original purchase is the RV's resale value. Naturally, choosing an RV that fits your needs right now should be your top priority, but knowing its depreciation rate and possible resale value will help you make a more informed purchase. Well-known brands with a solid track record of dependability and quality typically hold their worth better over time. You can see the long-term financial effects of your choice of RV model more clearly if you thoroughly investigate its resale value.

For long-term ownership, it is essential to comprehend the upkeep needs and probable repair expenses related to the particular kind of RV you have chosen. The maintenance requirements of different RVs might vary, so it's important to know what the manufacturer recommends for regular upkeep. To guarantee that you can handle maintenance needs quickly and effectively, consider the availability of repair facilities and replacement parts for your preferred RV. A more thorough evaluation of the total ownership experience is achieved by accounting for probable repair expenses and the convenience of receiving care.

Test driving or taking a tour of the selected model is an essential step in the RV purchasing process that is sometimes overlooked. You can evaluate the RV's overall comfort, maneuverability, and driving dynamics by taking it for a test drive. You may understand how well an RV fits your driving style and handling comfort by taking a test drive or pulling a travel trailer. Examining the RV's interior allows you to ensure that it satisfies your needs and standards for comfort while traveling by assessing its design, features, and general livability.

In summary, choosing the ideal RV for your trip is complex and requires a thorough evaluation of several criteria. Every factor, including the RV's size and kind, intended use, budget, and amenities, affects how well the vehicle fits your travel objectives. Ensuring the RV you choose works well with your lifestyle and serves as a foundation for unique and fun road trips requires careful consideration, test driving, and an awareness of your preferences. When you set out to choose the ideal recreational vehicle (RV), a thorough assessment of these variables will enable you to make an informed decision that will improve your trip by giving you the flexibility and comfort to see the world at your speed.

Route Planning and Itinerary Creation

Creating an itinerary and arranging routes are essential components of RV travel since they mold the trip and impact the whole open-road experience. Setting a route and making an itinerary requires striking a careful balance between spontaneity and planning, enabling tourists to enjoy the freedom of the open road and guaranteeing a comprehensive and pleasurable travel experience. Route planning necessitates a deliberate strategy considering travel preferences, time limits, and the desire to find hidden gems. This process starts with choosing the starting point and continues with figuring out the final destination and the spots in between.

Determining the RV trip's objective and aims is an essential component of route planning. Whether you're planning a cross-country expedition, a relaxing road trip, or an adventure through a national park, knowing the trip's main goals can help you create an agenda. A more flexible and open-ended itinerary would suit someone looking for a leisurely pace with plenty of opportunity for impromptu detours. However, those with specific places in mind—like famous national parks or critical historical sites—might choose a more regimented plan to ensure they see everything they want.

Choosing a beginning location is essential when arranging a route since it establishes the mood for the entire trip. Depending on personal preferences, this could be a well-known home base or an exciting new location that signifies the start of the voyage. The beginning place also affects the total itinerary, dictating the roads traveled, the terrain seen, and the variety of activities seen. Whether traveling from coast to coast or visiting a specific area, the beginning point is the first link in a carefully planned itinerary.

When travelers set out to arrange their itinerary, choosing their destinations becomes crucial. Beautiful roads, historic towns, national parks, and cultural sites all add to the diversity of an RV experience. Combining must-see sights with discoveries from the usual path ensures a thorough examination of the selected itinerary. Travelers can appreciate the distinctive features of every place, such as outdoor recreation, cultural events, and regional food, by doing extensive study on each one. Thanks to this knowledge, RV enthusiasts can customize their route to fit their interests and tastes.

The length of the RV trip significantly influences route planning and itinerary creation. The breadth and intricacy of the schedule are influenced by the amount of time available for travel, whether it's a quick weekend escape, a lengthy road trip, or a months-long adventure. Longer trips allow for the luxury of meandering itineraries and extended stays, enabling visitors to experience each place fully. On the other hand, shorter vacations call for a more concentrated strategy that emphasizes the most important sights and activities in a condensed amount of time. Finding the ideal balance between the trip's length and the program's intricacy guarantees a fulfilling and stress-free experience.

There's often a combination of driving days and long breaks in the rhythm of the road. A crucial part of route planning is figuring out the daily trip distance and pace, considering driving preferences, energy levels, and the desire to enjoy each stop fully. Some RV fans want a more leisurely pace with shorter journeys and longer stays at each destination, while others love the romance of the open road and may travel longer distances in a single day. An itinerary customized to individual comfort levels makes for a more pleasurable and environmentally friendly travel experience.

Weather and seasonal factors are essential when designing a route because they affect the itinerary's general design and the destinations chosen. Travelers can better prepare for varied situations by being aware of each place's climate and weather trends along the journey. For example, avoiding harsh weather, such as winter storms or intense summer heat, ensures safer and more enjoyable travel. Additionally, RV enthusiasts can maximize outdoor activities and natural features at each site by scheduling their routes to coincide with good seasons.

Today's RV travelers find that technology is an indispensable tool, providing information for creating itineraries and planning routes. Setting a route and finding areas of interest along the road is made easier with the help of navigation applications, internet mapping services, and trip planners explicitly designed for RVs. These applications improve the effectiveness and simplicity of route planning by offering real-time updates on traffic, road conditions, and neighboring facilities. When preparing, travelers can stay informed, flexible, and connected while traveling by utilizing technology.

A vital component of an enjoyable RV trip is still flexibility, which also applies to designing itineraries and routes. A well-planned itinerary guides the trip, but allowing for spontaneity enables visitors to take advantage of unforeseen chances and adjust to changing conditions. You might stumble upon a fellow RV enthusiast, attend a nearby festival, or be drawn to a charming wayside site. These are all enjoyable diversions that add to the entire experience. The voyage will flow naturally if structure and flexibility are balanced, making room for chance encounters and surprising discoveries.

A well-rounded and pleasurable itinerary must consider each trip partner's requirements and inclinations. Whether you're traveling alone, with a partner, or with your family, it's essential to consider everyone's varied interests and ensure everyone has a positive experience. Participatory planning meetings enable every traveler to offer suggestions, ideas, and personal preferences. This all-inclusive strategy encourages shared ownership in the journey, turning it into a group adventure that meets everyone's needs and interests.

During the whole route planning process, safety is the priority. Travelers' overall safety is improved when the route and itinerary are chosen to comply with safety standards and regulations. Avoiding unforeseen difficulties along the path is made more accessible by watching for potential dangers, construction updates, and road closures. Additionally, following suggested driving hours and planning rest periods into the schedule increases driver attention and reduces fatigue-related risks. Making safety a priority when creating a route helps ensure a safe and stress-free RV travel experience.

RV travelers may enrich their journey and embrace the spirit of exploration and discovery by exploring local activities and immersing themselves in each destination's culture. A more fulfilling and unforgettable travel experience is produced when authentic experiences, such as historical landmarks, regional food, and local markets and festivals, are incorporated into the itinerary. A more profound connection with the locations visited is facilitated by interacting with locals and enjoying the uniqueness of each stop, which enhances the quality of the RV trip as a whole.

To sum up, creating an itinerary and planning routes are essential to having a successful and pleasurable RV travel experience. Every detail must be carefully considered, from choosing the beginning point to figuring out the destinations, daily speed, and length of the trip. An itinerary that fits travel objectives and personal preferences is the result of careful planning, including integrating technology, striking the correct balance between structure and flexibility, and prioritizing safety. Ultimately, route planning mastery enables RV travelers to customize their trip and realize all of the open road's possibilities while making lifelong experiences.

Essential Gear and Supplies for RV Camping

A successful and pleasurable road trip starts with the necessary RV camping equipment and supplies. When vacationers set out on their RV travels, it becomes critical to carefully examine what gear they will need to provide comfort, security, and convenience all along the way. The choice and arrangement of equipment is essential to the preparation process; it ranges from necessities for setting up camp to tools and accessories that improve the whole RV experience.

A dependable leveling system is one of the essential pieces of gear needed when setting up camp. Ensuring the RV is level when parked is vital because this improves interior comfort and supports the efficient operation of the appliances and systems. When paired with a bubble level, leveling blocks or systems become essential for creating a level and sturdy campground.

Securing the RV in its designated spot is another crucial step in the camping setup process. Sturdy and dependable wheel chocks provide additional safety and stability by preventing accidental rolling or movement when parked. Purchasing high-quality chocks that are sized and weighed appropriately for the RV guarantees a stable base for the duration of the visit. Stabilizing jacks also help to reduce swaying and rocking, which improves the living area's overall comfort.

A well-made, long-lasting patio mat becomes a necessary piece of equipment for the outside living space. The mat accomplishes several goals by offering a tidy and cozy area outside the RV. It provides a specific space for outdoor activities, keeps dirt and dust at bay, and fosters a relaxing mood. Choosing a weather-resistant mat that is simple to clean will ensure its longevity and user-friendliness.

As anyone who enjoys the outdoors knows, having a sturdy pair of camping chairs is necessary to appreciate the environment entirely. For outdoor activities, folding chairs offer a comfortable seating option that is lightweight, portable, and easy to use. Sturdy camping chairs give a convenient and relaxing element to RV camping, whether you're lounging around the campfire, eating outside, or just soaking in the scenery.

The awning of the RV expands the living area outside, offering protection from the weather and shade. It becomes worthwhile to invest in awning accessories to utilize this function entirely. The adaptability of the awning is increased with attachable lighting, sunscreens, and wind deflectors, which create a welcoming outdoor area that can be adjusted to suit different tastes and weather conditions. These accessories enhance an outdoor living space that is more flexible and enjoyable.

Storage and organization options are essential for the RV to be as efficient and spacious as possible. Stackable bins, small organizers, and collapsible storage containers all aid in keeping stuff organized when driving and parking. RV aficionados may keep their living spaces neat and clutter-free by making the most of the storage areas in cabinets, closets, and beneath beds. Furthermore, securing goods with adjustable organizers and non-slip liners stops them from shifting while in transit, making the trip more orderly and seamless.

Kitchen necessities are an essential portion of the equipment and materials required for RV camping. Travelers may make meals quickly and enjoy the ease of home-cooked meals out on the road with the help of a well-equipped kitchen. Cookware sets with nesting pots and pans—ideal for small spaces—are essential kitchen appliances. Cutting boards, utensils, and kitchen tools designed specifically for RV use improve the cooking experience. Furthermore, a camping stove or portable grill broadens the cooking possibilities, enabling outdoor meal preparation and enhancing the dining experience.

A dependable and effective refrigerator is a vital component of an RV kitchen, offering sufficient space for preserving perishable goods while traveling. A refrigerator's overall functionality in an RV kitchen is enhanced by choosing one with the right size and features, like temperature controls and movable shelves. Furthermore, frozen foods can be stored in a small freezer section, allowing you to enjoy various meals without frequent grocery store trips.

A collection of sturdy trash bags, recycling bins, and compostable bags is crucial for waste management in RVs. Adhering to ethical camping principles, proper disposal, and recycling methods can help maintain a tidy and orderly living area. Trash compactors or containers with covers stop the smell and keep waste safe while in transit, guaranteeing a clean and ecologically responsible method of getting rid of garbage.

Having a set of dinnerware suitable for an RV, such as bowls, plates, and utensils, makes mealtimes more convenient. Travel-friendly and robust alternatives provide a comfortable and helpful way to eat while withstanding the rigors of the road, and choosing crockery that nests and stacks allow you to maximize RV storage space.

Access to drinkable water is a crucial factor in RV camping. Connecting to campground water sources is made easier with a sturdy water hose explicitly made for RV use, guaranteeing a consistent and secure water supply. Purchasing a water filter or purification system improves the quality of the water, giving you peace of mind when adding fresh water to the RV's tank or connecting to outside sources. Sufficient jugs and containers for storing water also help to ensure water efficiency when traveling.

The RV's plumbing system must be maintained carefully, and waste disposal depends on the appropriate sewage hose. A sturdy and flexible sewage hose with the right length and connectors ensures an efficient and safe connection to the RV's holding tanks and dump station facilities. Furthermore, sanitizing agents, disposable gloves, and a special hose for cleaning the black water tank all help to A hassle-free, sanitary method of managing garbage.

A dependable and continuous power supply is ensured by having the required electrical accessories, a crucial component of RV camping power management. The RV's electrical system is protected by various heavy-duty extension cords, adapters, and surge protectors, making it easy to connect to power sources at campgrounds. For off-grid camping, portable generators provide independence and campground flexibility as a backup power source.

An RV-specific toilet paper made for septic systems is essential to handle the always crucial topic of personal hygiene. RV-friendly toilet paper dissolves more readily than standard toilet paper, avoiding clogs and promoting effective waste removal. Shower caddies, organizers, and water-saving showerheads are small, lightweight shower accessories that help make bathing in the RV comfortable and water-efficient.

A dependable GPS intended for recreational vehicle use becomes a vital tool for road navigation. RV-specific GPS devices offer tailored routes that consider the vehicle's dimensions, mass, and height, assisting in avoiding low bridges, constrained roads, and other hazards. RV enthusiasts may travel with more excellent safety and confidence thanks to this technology, making navigating and getting where they're going easier.

Safety equipment is a must-have when RV camping, and guests should prioritize goods that increase security and emergency preparedness. One vital piece of safety equipment is a well-stocked first aid bag that includes necessary medical materials. Strategically positioned fire extinguishers within the recreational vehicle (RV) enhance fire safety, and smoke and carbon monoxide detectors offer timely alerts in an emergency. A dependable tool kit that contains all the instruments needed for RV upkeep and repairs provides an additional measure of preparation.

Having dependable lighting options is crucial for improving the evening and night outdoor experience. Enough illumination is provided around the campsite with LED lanterns, string lights, and headlamps, enhancing safety and visibility. Without relying on conventional power sources, solar-powered lights offer an environmentally and economically responsible alternative for outdoor illumination, enabling RV owners to take in the ambiance of their surroundings.

RV travelers' comfort and well-being are enhanced by wearing and carrying equipment and clothing appropriate for the weather, especially when visiting different regions and climates. Gear such as sun protection items, hiking boots with good support, waterproof jackets, and layered clothes guarantee that travelers are ready for any weather. In addition, carrying necessities like sunscreen, bug repellent, and a small travel umbrella increases the outdoor experience's adaptability.

To sum up, basic supplies and equipment for RV camping include a wide variety of products that support roadside comfort, security, and convenience. Every piece of equipment is essential to the RV experience, from leveling systems and wheel chocks for setting up camp to patio rugs and camping chairs for maximizing outdoor living areas. Kitchen necessities, waste management options, power and electrical accessories, and safety equipment enhance a well-planned and enjoyable trip. After carefully selecting their equipment and supplies, RV aficionados head off, knowing they are ready for their adventures. They embrace the freedom of living in an RV and make lifelong memories.

CHAPTER III

Navigating America's National Treasures

Overview of Iconic National Parks

The famous national parks dispersed around the nation serve as monuments to the stunning and varied landscapes of the United States, home to a fantastic assortment of natural treasures. These protected areas, meant to highlight and conserve the nation's natural beauty, bring in millions of tourists annually with their breathtaking landscapes, distinctive ecosystems, and outdoor leisure options. A summary of some of the most well-known national parks offers an insight into the exceptional beauty and biological diversity that define these priceless environments.

California's Yosemite National Park is well-known for its massive granite cliffs, gushing waterfalls, and old sequoia trees. El Capitan and Half Dome, two of Yosemite's most famous landmarks, have earned the park's designation as a World Heritage Site. The park has a wide range of plant and animal life due to its different ecosystems, which range from beautiful meadows to deep woods. Visitors can fully experience Yosemite's grandeur via hiking trails, rock climbing routes, and picturesque drives. Notable locations like Yosemite Valley and Glacier Point also provide incredible panoramic views.

The first national park in the world is Yellowstone National Park, which is located in Wyoming, Montana, and Idaho. Yellowstone was created in 1872 and is well- known for its geothermal marvels, including the Old Faithful geyser. The enormous nature of the park has a wide variety of environments, from deep canyons to alpine meadows. This protected area is home to various wildlife, including wolves, bison, elk, and grizzly bears. The largest high-elevation lake in North America, Yellowstone Lake, enhances the park's attraction by offering a tranquil contrast to the geothermal characteristics.

The Grand Canyon National Park in Arizona symbolizes nature's overwhelming grandeur. With its striking depths, brilliant colors, and intricately stratified rock formations, the Grand Canyon is a captivating sight, sculpted over millions of years by the Colorado River. Most visitors congregate along the South Rim, which features famous vantage spots like Yavapai Observation Station and Mather Point. Hikers who are feeling adventurous can go along paths such as Bright Angel and South Kaibab into the canyon to get a closer look at this natural wonder.

Zion National Park in Utah entices visitors with its lush Zion Canyon, slot canyons, and majestic sandstone cliffs. A beautiful oasis is created in the middle of the harsh landscape by the Virgin River as it flows through the park. Renowned for its strenuous hiking paths, Zion is home to the well-known Angel's Landing and The Narrows. Beautiful vistas can be reached via the Zion-Mount Carmel Highway, and travelers can enjoy the park's splendor from the luxury of their cars on the Zion Canyon Scenic Drive.

With more than 2,000 naturally occurring stone arches, Utah's Arches National Park is home to a fantastic array of grotesque geological sculptures and red rock formations. With its graceful freestanding design, Delicate Arch has come to represent the park. Visitors can discover the park's delights on simple walks, breathtaking drives, or more strenuous routes like the Devil's Garden. Arches National Park becomes a stunning palette of hues as the sun sets over the fiery- hued rocks, making for a magical and unforgettable experience.

Bounding both North Carolina and Tennessee, the Great Smoky Mountains National Park is well-known for its mist-covered mountains, thick forests, and abundant wildlife. The Great Smoky Mountains, the most popular national park in the country, enthrall visitors with their otherworldly beauty. Hikers can experience the park's many landscapes as the Appalachian Trail passes. Cades Cove is a gorgeous valley with mountains in the background that offers chances to see wildlife and explore old buildings.

Colorado's Rocky Mountain National Park is a refuge for those who enjoy the outdoors and the mountains. With its stunning lakes, alpine meadows, and towering mountain peaks as its backdrop, the park is a great place to go hiking, wildlife viewing, and take beautiful drives. Offering stunning vistas of the Rocky Mountains, Trail Ridge Road is the highest continually paved road in the United States. The park's entrance towns, Estes Park and Grand Lake, provide quaint amenities that let guests unwind and rejuvenate.

Alaska's Denali National Park and Preserve, home to the magnificent Denali, the tallest peak in North America, displays the vast and untamed environment of the state. The six million acres of the park are home to tundra, glaciers, and a variety of habitats that are home to a wide variety of species, including wolves, moose, and grizzly bears. Although Denali's imposing presence is the main attraction, there are many possibilities for exploration and adventure thanks to the park's varied landscapes and vast route network.

The vast and distinctive wetland ecology of F orida's Everglades National Park is known as the "River of Grass." The park's various habitats include mangrove forests, sawgrass plains, and freshwater sloughs. The Everglades, home to many animals such as manatees, alligators, and different bird species, highlight the significance of protecting fragile ecosystems. Visitors can experience the park through boat tours, hiking trails, and wildlife viewing spots.

Granite peaks, rocky beaches, and thick forests characterize the breathtaking coastal region of Maine's Acadia National Park. The tallest peak on the East Coast, Cadillac Mountain, provides expansive views of the neighboring islands and the Atlantic Ocean. In addition to the famous Jordan Pond and Sand Beach, which entice tourists with their unspoiled beauty, Acadia's carriage roads offer a network of picturesque pathways for cyclists and hikers.

Some of the most significant trees in the world may be found in California's Sequoia and Kings Canyon National Parks, including the famous General Sherman Tree. The green spaces they are frequently run in tandem and feature the magnificent Giant Forest, where towering sequoias provide a splendid canopy. Hiking paths take hikers through various environments including verdant meadows and craggy canyons. The parks also have underground attractions ,such as Crystal Cave , which offers a fantastic look into the underground world.

Together, these recognizable national parks—each with its distinct personality and array of natural wonders— reflect the diverse fabric of American landscapes. Travelers who journey across the nation to discover these protected sites add to the heritage of conservation and appreciation of the exceptional beauty located within the boundaries of these national treasures. To ensure that the majesty of America's natural wonders is accessible and appreciated for years to come, preserving the diversity of ecosystems, geological formations, and wildlife habitats that these parks showcase is crucial.

Lesser-Known Gems Worth Exploring

Millions of people visit famous national parks each year. Still, there is a world of lesser-known treasures around the country that entice travelers with unique allure and undiscovered beauties. These lesser-known locations provide a more sedate and private experience, allowing travelers to escape the crowd and uncover the less-known aspects of the nation's varied topography. These lesser-known gems, which range from remote natural wonders to historic treasures, are well worth the trip for anyone looking for a more genuine and intimate relationship with the beauty that America has to offer.

With its variety of volcanic landscapes and geothermal wonders, Lassen Volcanic National Park in Northern California is a tribute to the unadulterated power of nature. Boiling springs, hissing fumaroles, and active geothermal zones create an unearthly atmosphere throughout the park. Bumpass Hell, a geothermal basin with bubbling springs, fumaroles, and colorful pools, is the main attraction. The southernmost active volcano in the Cascade Range, Lassen Peak, provides breathtaking views of the surrounding landscape. Despite its distinctive features and geological significance, Lassen Volcanic National Park is not well-known. This allows visitors to enjoy its captivating scenery without the crowds that come with visiting more popular parks.

Nevada's Great Basin National Park is a hidden treasure that beckons adventurers into a varied and challenging landscape. High alpine scenery and low desert basins are contrasted in this park, home to the snow-capped peaks of Wheeler Peak and old bristlecone pine trees. Beautiful vistas may be found on the Wheeler Peak Scenic Drive, while hiking routes like the Alpine Lakes and Bristlecone paths allow for exploration. With their distinctive formations, the Lehman Caves give the park's attractions an underground dimension. Great Basin National Park is a peaceful haven for individuals seeking isolation and the appeal of unspoiled scenery because of its relatively isolated position.

Georgia's Cumberland Island National Seashore is a stunning sanctuary on the Atlantic Coast known for its unspoiled beaches, marine forests, and historical landmarks. This barrier island, which can only be reached by ferry, is a tranquil getaway where guests can explore more than 50 miles of hiking trails, see wild horses galloping around, and see the remains of the Carnegie family's Dungeness mansion. Compared to the more well-known beach resorts, Cumberland Island's pristine beauty, with its marshes, dunes, and varied ecosystems, presents a unique chance to get in touch with nature in a peaceful coastal setting.

Utah's Capitol Reef National Park is a hidden gem known for its imposing monoliths, vibrant canyons, and remarkable geological formations. An almost 100-mile-long stretch in the Earth's crust called the Waterpocket Fold produces a panorama of bridges, domes, and cliffs. Enjoy breathtaking Goosenecks, Capitol Dome, and Chimney Rock views from the park's scenic road. The Cathedral Valley loop leads hikers through a secluded and enchanting park area with spires and monoliths that inspire awe and isolation. In the center of Utah's red rock area, Capitol Reef offers a more sedate and reflective experience because it receives fewer people than its more well-known cousins.

South Carolina's Congaree National Park is a hidden treasure located in the floodplains of the Congaree River. The park is a haven for biodiversity and is home to one of the world's tallest canopies of deciduous forests. A system of boardwalks and pathways that wind through marshes, bottomland hardwood forests, and old-growth hardwood woods can be explored by visitors. Canoeing and kayaking on the Congaree River allow visitors to see the park's distinctive scenery from a fresh angle. For those looking for a quiet getaway in the great outdoors, Congaree National Park is still a lesser-known gem because of its verdant surroundings, wide variety of species, and serene streams.

In California, the Lava Beds National Monument is an underground paradise that hides a complex system of caverns and lava tubes created by long-ago volcanic activity. More than 700 caverns are in the park, providing chances for subsurface exploration and discovery. Explore the caverns, take in the striking geological structures, and take in the peace of the underground environment. The monument also features historical battlegrounds, high-desert Modoc Plateau scenery, and Native American rock art. For those who are interested in the historical significance of volcanic landscapes and the riddles of geology, Lava Beds National Monument offers an intriguing and unusual travel experience.

Only accessible by ferry or seaplane, the secluded and immaculate archipelago of Michigan's Isle Royale National Park is in Lake Superior. This island wilderness may have a distinctive combination of craggy topography, boreal forests, and immaculate lakeshores. Backcountry hiking and camping on Isle Royale are well known for offering an immersive experience in a pristine natural setting. Trails that lead to picturesque vistas, secluded bays, and the ruins of former copper mining operations are open for exploration by tourists. For those looking for an unspoiled wilderness experience away from the beaten road, the park's remoteness and restricted accessibility add to its natural splendor.

The Texas Guadalupe Mountains National Park reveals the untamed splendor of the Guadalupe Mountains while providing a sanctuary for hikers and environment lovers. Guadalupe Point, Texas' tallest point, and a variety of topography, including canyons and vast stretches of high desert, are all included in the park. Hiking routes offering expansive views, such as the Devil's Hall Trail and the Guadalupe Peak Trail, are demanding but rewarding. El Capitan, the park's ancient petrified reef, enhances its attraction on a geological level. Guadalupe

Mountains National Park is a hidden gem for anyone looking for seclusion and the excitement of high- elevation adventure because of its vast panoramas and uncrowded routes.

The alpine splendor of Washington's North Cascades National Park is home to glaciers, deep woods, and rugged peaks. The park, also called the "American Alps," boasts a clean and mountainous scenery that rivals its more well-known counterparts. A system of paths that lead to alpine lakes, waterfalls, and overlooks displaying the park's striking landscape are open for exploration by visitors. The North Cascades Highway offers a breathtaking drive through its center, showcasing the park's many ecosystems and majestic mountain ranges. North Cascades National Park offers a tranquil getaway into the splendor of the Pacific Northwest due to its comparatively lower attendance than other national parks.

Often eclipsed by its neighbor Arches, Utah's Canyonlands National Park covers enormous valleys sculpted by the Colorado River and is a mesmerizing location. The park has four districts, each with unique recreational activities and sceneries. Towering spires and arches can be seen in the Needles area, while expansive mesa views can be found on the Island in the Sky district. For daring explorers, The Maze, one of the most isolated places in the country, provides a genuine wilderness experience. Experience the quiet and beauty of the Colorado Plateau in Canyonlands National Park, which boasts different scenery and fewer crowds.

Discoverers are drawn to these lesser-known jewels dispersed throughout the nation by their wild beauty, historical relevance, and distinctive ecosystems. While the country's famous national parks highlight its many wonders, these lesser-known gems offer a more intimate and sedate way to experience the many landscapes that make up the country. Discovering the underground caverns of Lava Beds National Monument, trekking the secluded paths of Isle Royale, or taking in the breathtaking geological structures of Capitol Reef, each of these experiences

Guidelines for Responsible RV Camping in National Parks

Maintaining these beloved sites' natural beauty and ecological integrity through responsible RV camping is essential. With RV travel becoming increasingly popular, enthusiasts must follow rules that reduce their environmental effects and encourage sustainable camping. Because of their delicate habitats and varied ecosystems, national parks demand careful management to guarantee that RV camping is a fun and low-impact activity for current and future generations.

Respecting Leave No Trace guidelines is essential for responsible RV camping in national parks. These guidelines stress the importance of reducing human influence on the environment by preserving cultural and natural elements in their original locations. Recreational vehicle tourists' goal is to leave campgrounds in as good of a state as when they arrived. This entails clearing up all litter, appropriately disposing of waste, and protecting the habitats of wildlife and plants. RV travelers can appreciate the splendor of national parks within the framework provided by Leave No Trace guidelines, which also honor the fragile ecosystems they pass through.

Choosing a campsite is essential to responsible RV camping. RVs can be accommodated at specially designated campgrounds found in many national parks. Selecting well-established campsites reduces the environmental effect because these locations are made especially to accommodate tourists. It is not advisable for RVers to build new campsites or go off-road because these actions might cause habitat disturbances for wildlife, erosion of the soil, and harm to plants. To protect the natural integrity of national parks and guarantee that future generations can enjoy magnificent landscapes, it is recommended that visitors stick to specified routes and camp in approved places.

Responsible garbage management is an essential component of ethical RV camping in national parks. Travelers in RVs should have the equipment to properly dispose of waste, such as trash, wastewater, and sewage. National parks usually have designated dump sites to dispose of RV garbage. It is essential to follow these facilities. Unauthorized rubbish disposal in areas like rivers or the ground presents severe environmental risks and jeopardizes national park conservation efforts. Responsible RV camping requires locating dump sites in advance and following correct waste disposal guidelines to protect the ecosystems.

Another essential rule for responsible RV camping is water conservation. Many national parks are situated in arid areas with scarce water supplies. RV owners should practice waste minimization and know how much water they use. This includes using water-saving gadgets, quickly addressing leaks, and maintaining appropriate personal hygiene and dishwashing practices. Water consumption limits may apply in some national parks; RV enthusiasts should become aware of these rules to ensure they are followed. In addition to protecting a valuable resource, prudent water management enhances the viability of RV camping in national parks as a whole.

An essential ethical factor for RV camping in national parks is respect for species and their habitats. RV enthusiasts are drawn to the appeal of seeing wildlife in their native habitats, but it's essential to observe these animals from a safe and considerate distance. Overly close contact with wildlife or attempts to feed them can negatively impact their survival instincts, behavior, and overall health. RV visitors should become informed of the restrictions governing wildlife watching in national parks to guarantee peaceful cohabitation with the park's wildlife. Keeping a respectful distance, observing through binoculars, and not interfering with natural behaviors are all ways to support healthy wildlife populations.

The peace and natural soundscape of national parks can be significantly impacted by noise pollution. Reducing noise levels is part of responsible RV camping to maintain the tranquility of these spaces. RVers should respect quiet hours, usually set forth by park laws, and refrain from making excessive noise that can annoy nearby campers or wildlife. To further reduce their influence on the tranquility of the environment, generator use ought to be restricted to specific times. RVers help to preserve the natural soundscape that gives national parks their distinct character by adopting a thoughtful and sensitive attitude to noise.

Responsible fire management is essential since many national parks are prone to wildfires. RV users should abide by the rules and regulations regarding fire set forth by park officials. This entails avoiding starting open fires in forbidden locations and utilizing grills or fire rings for cooking and campfires. Before visiting a national park, check for any fire bans or restrictions to ensure the current rules are followed. RV enthusiasts should also be mindful of the possible fire hazards connected to their activities and proceed with caution while discarding cigarette butts. In addition to enhancing park safety, prudent fire control shields these ecosystems from the destructive effects of wildfires.

An essential component of responsible RV camping is familiarizing oneself with every national park s unique rules and regulations. Rules in national parks may differ according to their distinct ecosystems, animal populations, and topography. RV travelers should spend some time getting acquainted with the rules of the parks they intend to visit, whether they have to do with camping permissions, seeing wildlife, hiking, or other activities. Maintaining awareness of and adherence to park regulations guarantees a peaceful visit and contributes to preserving the delicate ecosystem balance of each national park.

Encouragement of eco-friendly and sustainable practices is a general rule covering many facets of responsible RV camping. This entails forming eco-aware behaviors like using biodegradable soaps, cutting back on energy use, and selecting eco-friendly goods. RV users can reduce their carbon footprint by using solar energy, driving more fuel-efficiently, and using environmentally friendly camping methods. The general objective of maintaining the natural beauty and ecological health of national parks is in line with being aware of one's environmental impact and looking for ways to lessen it.

Traveling responsibly and ethically means considering cultural and communal factors in addition to personal behavior. RV travelers expect respect for local populations, their customs, and the cultural legacy of the regions around national parks. RV enthusiasts can foster positive relationships with the areas they visit by being mindful of locals, patronizing local businesses, and participating in local events. Leaving a positive legacy for these beloved locations' local populations and the environment is critical to ethical tourism.

To sum up, leaving no trace principles, thoughtful campsite selection, waste management, water conservation, respect for wildlife, noise reduction, fire management, park regulations education, and sustainable practices are all essential components of responsible RV camping in national parks. RVers help to preserve the national parks' scenic splendor, biological richness, and cultural value by adhering to these rules. The intention is to foster peaceful cohabitation between RVers and these priceless environments to preserve the allure of national parks for future generations.

CHAPTER IV

Setting Up Camp

Choosing the Perfect Campsite

A vital component of the outdoor experience is choosing the ideal campground, which sets the stage for unforgettable activities and ensures a cozy and pleasurable stay. Selecting a campsite significantly impacts the entire camping experience, whether you're going on a multi-day backpacking trip through the backcountry or staying at a campground with all the facilities you could ever need. Several considerations must be carefully considered before making this choice, including the desired isolation level, safety, topography, and location. A well-selected campground fosters sustainability, improves one's relationship with the natural world, and makes camping enjoyable for all campers.

The location of a campsite within the designated camping area is the first factor to be considered. The accessibility of services like water supplies, trash disposal sites, and restrooms may be a top concern for campers in well-established campgrounds. Families with young children or people with special needs may choose campsites near these amenities to ensure convenience. Backcountry campers looking for seclusion and a more intense encounter with nature could favor locations farther away from populated areas. The campsite's location determines the whole camping experience by deciding how much immersion is in the natural environment and how much self-sufficiency is needed.

When choosing a campsite, terrain is an essential factor to consider. For tent setup and comfortable sleeping, a level and well-drained platform is necessary. Areas that are prone to floods or have a sharp inclination that could endanger their comfort and safety should be avoided by campers. Selecting a campsite with soft ground, like grass or pine needles, also improves the whole camping experience. Rocky or uneven terrain might make it challenging to put up equipment and make sleeping uncomfortable. By carefully evaluating the terrain, campers may guarantee a more comfortable and pleasurable camping experience.

A campsite's safety is the most crucial factor to take into account. Campers should be mindful of any potential risks in the vicinity, such as flooding, wildlife activity, or falling limbs. While it is beneficial to be near water sources, camping too close to rivers or streams puts you in danger of flooding, particularly during erratic weather. It is easier for campers to decide whether or not their selected location is safe when they are aware of potential hazards, such as fallen trees or unstable rock formations. Respecting wildlife habitats, staying out of fragile ecosystems, and reducing human disturbance are other ways that follow the Leave No Trace philosophy, which helps to protect the environment and ensure camper safety.

Determining the ideal degree of seclusion is one of the most critical factors in selecting the perfect campsite. Choose a location away from busy streets and well-traveled paths if you want a peaceful and isolated experience. Backcountry campers may explore farther into the forest in search of remote areas that provide a closer, more intimate experience with the natural world. However, those who want a more social setting could choose to camp in well-established campgrounds where they are more likely to engage with other campers. Finding the perfect campground depends on personal preferences and the kind of camping experience desired, and it often involves striking a balance between the need for privacy and social features as well as accessibility.

Weather is a significant factor in the selection process when choosing a campsite. The general comfort and security of camping are improved by shaded areas and shielded from the wind and rain. Selecting a campsite that minimizes exposure to the elements makes it more accessible for campers by understanding probable weather changes and prevailing wind patterns during the camping season. Finding natural windbreaks in the form of thick vegetation or other topographical features also makes camping more comfortable and safe. Camping responsibly and having fun requires adjusting to shifting weather patterns and selecting a location that provides shelter from the elements.

A crucial component of ethical camping is limiting the environmental impact, and choosing a campground is essential to achieving this goal. Choosing campsites that have already been formed, avoiding developing new sites, and reducing trampling on plants are all part of the Leave No Trace philosophy. We may protect delicate ecosystems and avoid needless environmental harm by choosing sturdy surfaces, such as well-trod paths or authorized camping locations. Through thoughtful campground selection and reduced human disturbance, campers help preserve the outdoor environments they are fortunate to experience.

When choosing a campsite, water availability is crucial, especially for people who want to fish, kayak, or swim— all outdoor activities that depend on a water source. Being close to water makes obtaining a necessary resource for cleaning, cooking, and staying hydrated easy. But campers also need to follow the rules for responsible water use and consider their influence on the ecosystem. When choosing a location near water, one must consider flood hazards, possible variations in water levels, and the necessity of leaving no trace to preserve aquatic ecosystems.

Permits and regulations are crucial elements that affect the choice of campground. There are tight rules around camping in many places, particularly in national parks and wilderness areas. These rules may include group size limitations, designated camping zones, and permit requirements. To ensure compliance and avoid any disturbances to the camping experience, campers should become familiar with the rules and regulations of the region they have chosen. The sustainability and preservation of natural environments are enhanced by obtaining the required licenses and abiding by set rules.

Accessibility is a factor that changes based on personal preferences and needs. Accessibility elements in campgrounds or proximity to parking places may be crucial for individuals with mobility impairments. RVs and trailers are specialized equipment therefore campers should select locations that can comfortably fit their cars. Accessibility is balanced with other considerations, including privacy and security, to guarantee that every camper, no matter what their needs, can have a customized camping experience.

In summary, selecting the ideal campground is a complex process that considers several factors, including topography, accessibility, safety, seclusion, weather, availability of water, rules, and environmental impact. Every element counts, as it determines the comfort and safety of the selected location, the degree of absorption in nature, and the entire camping experience. Campers may improve their outdoor experiences, help preserve natural areas, and guarantee that future generations can appreciate the splendor of the great outdoors by choosing their campsites carefully and wisely.

Tips for Efficient RV Setup

Both seasoned travelers and novices can benefit from knowing how to set up an RV efficiently. It improves the whole camping experience and makes the transition from the open road to a cozy home on wheels seamless. An RV's setup entails several steps, such as leveling the car, connecting the utilities, and designing a comfortable and valuable living area. RV enthusiasts can simplify and improve the setup process with meticulous preparation, organization, and attention to detail. These pointers cover everything from leveling to utility connections to outside considerations and interior organization, offering a thorough how-to for making the most of an RV camping trip.

Leveling the vehicle is an essential first step in RV setup that improves comfort and safety. Uneven ground can make it difficult to sleep, interfere with appliance performance, and even cause damage to the RV's interior. A stable and level position can be attained by placing leveling blocks or pads beneath the RV's wheels. When altering the RV's position, it is best to use a bubble level or leveling application to ensure accuracy. Stabilizer jack deployment improves stability even more for motorized RV owners and minimizes movement when the passengers are inside. Campers can make their camping experience more pleasant and pleasurable by leveling the RV precisely.

Utility hookups, including water, electricity, and sewer lines, are essential for an RV setup. Utilizing a pressure regulator when connecting to a campground's water supply is advised to safeguard the RV's plumbing from overly high water pressure. A water filter can also enhance the quality of the water and keep impurities out of the RV's system. A good surge protector should be used to protect appliances and electronic equipment from power fluctuations while making electrical connections. Preventing electrical problems requires correctly ensuring the power source is connected to the campground and monitoring the voltage. Using a sewer hose support when connecting to a sewer helps keep the flow steady and avoids backups. Sewer hookups can be made hygienic and hassle-free by using gloves and adhering to sanitary procedures.

External factors greatly influence RV configuration for comfort and safety. Having an outside living area improves the camping trip as a whole. Awnings, outside furniture, and creating a unique space for cooking or lounging can all help achieve this. Using outdoor rugs or mats, you may reduce dirt tracking into your RV and maintain a clean campsite. Placing the RV to optimize shade while considering the sun's direction at various times is another aspect of creating a clever outdoor arrangement. Campers expand their living area outside the RV and strengthen their bond with the natural world by designing a cozy and functional outdoor space.

A crucial component of an effective RV setup is interior organization, which enhances accessibility and comfort. Setting aside necessities commonly needed during setup, like outside accessories, utility connections, and leveling tools, in order of importance guarantees quick access when needed. It is best to store goods safely while traveling to avoid shifting and possible damage. Keeping stuff organized and making the most of the limited space are achieved using bins, organizers, and storage solutions for RVs. Putting a checklist for the setup process that covers things like sliding out, extending awnings, and inspecting equipment guarantees a systematic and exhaustive procedure. Campers can improve their RV camping experience by creating a comfortable and valuable living space by cultivating an orderly interior.

Optimizing the kitchen arrangement is one area of interior organization that makes a big difference in RV living efficiency. Organization is essential to guarantee simple meal preparation and a pleasurable cooking experience in a small kitchen. Use foldable kitchen utensils, multipurpose appliances, and stackable cookware to maximize storage space. Putting a meal planning technique into practice and keeping basic pantry supplies stocked lessens the frequency of grocery store visits. Cooking is streamlined when the kitchen is set up according to usage patterns and meal prep procedures. Using outdoor cooking alternatives, such as camp stoves or portable barbecues, increases cooking options and offers flexibility. Cooking while traveling may be a delightful experience for RV enthusiasts who set up a functional and tidy kitchen.

Efficient RV setup also includes the bedroom, where furnishing a cozy and peaceful environment is crucial for a restful night's sleep. Purchasing high-quality mattresses and bedding that fit the RV's size will improve the quality of your sleep and your comfort level overall. Storage options like overhead cabinets or under-bed storage bins keep the bedroom space neat and clutter-free. Campers can customize the ambiance to their liking by using blackout curtains or shades while improving privacy and controlling natural light. Putting together a peaceful and unique bedroom arrangement adds to the RV's overall feeling of comfort and home.

Another essential component of practical RV life is bathroom setup, which requires meticulous planning and upkeep. During the camping trip, annoyance can be avoided by ensuring the RV's bathroom is adequately supplied with necessities, such as toilet paper and toiletries that are appropriate for an RV. Shower caddies and organizers are two examples of storage solutions that maximize the tiny space in the bathroom while maintaining easy access to objects. A clean and functioning bathroom setup requires routine maintenance, which includes cleaning the shower and toilet. Efficiency and sustainability are enhanced by using water-saving showerheads and sparingly using water. RV campers may have all the conveniences of home on the road without compromising comfort by making the most of their bathroom arrangement.

A well-rounded and pleasurable vacation is ensured by including efficient entertainment and connectivity installations, improving the overall RV camping experience. Strategically placing entertainment devices, such as TVs or audio systems, in the RV facilitates ideal viewing or listening experiences and user flexibility. Incorporating technological solutions, such as mobile hotspots or Wi-Fi boosters, enables campers to maintain connectivity even in isolated areas. Cable and cord organization keeps things tidy and facilitates the assembly and disassembly of entertainment equipment —an accessible and well-organized electronics setup benefits from creating specific areas for gadgets and charging stations. Campers can combine leisure and adventure with an RV experience with entertainment and connectivity options.

A thorough approach to effective RV setup considers safety precautions to provide a safe and worry-free camping trip. For camper safety, it is imperative to regularly inspect vital safety elements like carbon monoxide, smoke, and propane alarms. Awareness of the locations and methods of use of safety devices, such as emergency exits and fire extinguishers, helps one be ready for unforeseen circumstances. Accidents are reduced by using secure storage solutions, and shifting during travel is prevented for heavy or possibly hazardous objects. RV campers can enjoy their trips with peace of mind if they prioritize safety as an essential component of the setup procedure.

A crucial component of an effective setup is adjusting to the unique characteristics of the RV and its systems. Avoiding needless delays and disappointments can be achieved by being familiar with the user handbook of the RV and learning how to operate the slide-outs, awnings, and other features. Campers should conduct a pre-trip checklist that includes all setup duties to stay organized and ensure that all critical stages are noticed. Adopting a proactive, systematic strategy

Setting up duties helps people feel competent and confident, especially if they are new to RV camping. Those who take the time to become familiar with the RV's features and configuration can maximize their travel time and have no trouble getting around.

To sum up, setting up a practical RV requires careful thought for a variety of factors, including leveling, utility connections, exterior considerations, interior organization, kitchen setup, comfort in the bedroom, bathroom efficiency, entertainment and connectivity, safety precautions, and customization for the particular features of the RV. Each element enhances the comfort, accessibility, and pleasure of the camping experience as a whole. RV enthusiasts may maximize their living space, speed up the setup process, and go on memorable trips, knowing that their mobile home is well-thought-out and ready for any adventure by implementing these recommendations into their daily routine.

Creating a Comfortable Outdoor Living Space

Creating a comfortable outdoor living space is a transformative endeavor that elevates the camping experience, turning the surrounding nature into an extension of one's home. The outdoor living space provides a haven for campers to unwind, eat, and commune with nature, whether camping in an RV, tent, or beneath the stars. The careful selection of furnishings, lighting, cooking stations, and personal touches enhances the mood and usefulness of this area. The idea is to create an atmosphere of ease and leisure so that campers may completely appreciate the natural surroundings while indulging in the amenities of a well- thought-out outdoor living area.

Choosing the right furniture is essential to creating a cozy and welcoming outdoor living area. Foldable chairs, collapsible tables, and inflatable loungers are sound choices for campers who use tents. These items are lightweight and movable. Campers may consider investing in more substantial furniture, such as small outdoor sofas or dining sets, in RVs, where space may be more plentiful. Comfort is guaranteed for extended usage periods with high-quality camping chairs with robust construction and ergonomic designs. Furthermore, extending outdoor furniture's lifespan with weather-resistant and sturdy materials ensures dependable comfort for many camping excursions. The furniture arrangement in an outdoor living room should consider the surrounding natural environment, maximize vistas, and promote an air of openness.

Lighting serves more purposes in an outdoor living area than just providing illumination; it also sets the mood and improves the entire camping experience. In addition to providing illumination, string lights, lanterns, and LED fixtures also help create a warm and welcoming atmosphere. Solar-powered lighting is an environmentally responsible solution that provides lighting without using conventional power sources. Camping becomes more magical when lights are placed thoughtfully across the grounds, like long walks or draped over tent lines. Dimmable lanterns and other adjustable lighting options offer adaptability and let campers customize the environment. When night falls and the sun sets, well-chosen lighting turns the outdoor living area into a peaceful haven.

The outdoor living space's cooking settings are essential to the camping experience because they create a social atmosphere and make cooking delectable meals surrounded by nature possible. For campers who enjoy cooking, portable grills, camp stoves, and small kitchen setups are necessities. Outdoor kitchens with counter space and cooking appliances are a practical addition to indoor cooking areas for RV lovers. Meal prep efficiency is increased when cooking tools, pots, and pans are arranged conveniently and compactly. To further enhance the usability of the outdoor living area, a dedicated dining area with a collapsible table and cozy chairs should be established. Combining the cooking and dining areas creates a central area where campers may congregate, tell tales, and enjoy alfresco dining.

The outdoor living area becomes more unique and reflects the camper's tastes and personality when it is personalized. A cozy and comfortable ambiance can be created by bringing personal objects like blankets, toss pillows, or even a favorite outdoor rug. Outdoor artwork, lanterns, and flags are a few examples of decorations with a camping theme that give the area personality. Customization also includes the selection of outdoor pursuits, such as assembling a carry-along hammock for lazy afternoons or adding a telescope for stargazing. Campers can express themselves freely in the outdoor living area, which gives them a sense of pride and a bond with their makeshift home in the woods.

Considering shade and shelter is essential to designing a cozy outdoor living area that provides protection from the weather and guarantees a pleasurable camping trip in various weather scenarios. Awnings, pop-up tents, and canopies offer protection from sudden downpours and shade on bright days. Picking a campground with natural shade, such as beneath a tree canopy, improves comfort and shields against intense heat for tent campers. Adding a foldable umbrella or purchasing a multipurpose camping gazebo increases the outdoor living area's adaptability. In addition to being functional, shade improves comfort levels and tempts campers to spend more time outside without fear of the damaging effects of the sun.

Simple ground coverings or more ornate outdoor rugs or mats are available as flooring solutions for the outdoor living area. Ground coverings offer a comfortable platform for walking while shielding against damp or uneven surfaces. Outdoor rugs define particular regions within the outdoor living area, such as the dining or lounging zones, and provide a layer of warmth and aesthetic appeal to the environment. For tent campers, portable flooring options are beneficial because they provide insulation from the cold ground and keep dampness and dirt out of the living area. The flooring selection enhances the outdoor space's overall design and use, transforming it into a cozy and well-defined addition to the camping setup.

Having a well-organized and clutter-free outdoor living space requires storage solutions. Foldable containers, organizers explicitly designed for camping, and storage boxes allow campers to minimize visual clutter while keeping necessities close at hand. Outdoor storage compartments or mounted racks offer specific areas for tools, outdoor equipment, and camping supplies for RV campers. Maintaining a regular tidy-up schedule and setting up separate spaces for storage for belongings help streamline the setup process and keep the outdoor living area from being too big for use. Organizing also includes waste management; campers use specially designed bins for trash and recyclables to keep the atmosphere tidy and environmentally friendly.

With activities for leisure and relaxation, entertainment alternatives enhance the outdoor living area and bring something new to enjoy. A dynamic and convivial atmosphere can be created with board games, portable speakers, or musical instruments. For those looking for a more tranquil and lonely experience, there are books, e-readers, and nature guides available. Adding a portable projector to your backyard movie evenings or stargazing events expands your evening entertainment options. Incorporating outdoor pursuits like hiking, birdwatching, or stargazing into the living area can foster a connection between campers and the surrounding natural beauty. By adding entertainment alternatives, you can make the outdoor living space a lively and adaptable space that suits different tastes and moods.

Developing a comfortable outdoor living area requires careful attention to the environment, focusing on sustainable methods that reduce disturbance of the surrounding ecosystem. Reusable or environmentally appropriate outdoor dinnerware reduces waste and makes camping a more sustainable activity. Choosing solar-powered devices and lights reduces dependency on conventional power sources and throwaway batteries. Responsible trash management, including recycling and effective litter disposal, ensures the preservation of the natural environment for future campers. Respecting the Leave No Trace guidelines, which include reducing human disturbance of plants and wildlife, promotes a positive rapport between campers and the environment. Campers voluntarily contribute to preserving the outdoor environments they value by implementing sustainable practices.

In summary, designing a cozy outdoor living area is a dynamic and individualized project that blends functionality, style, and a sense of connection to the natural world. Campers can make their camping area a cozy and well-balanced extension of their home by carefully selecting furnishings, lighting, cooking sets, personalizing, shade and shelter, flooring alternatives, storage solutions, entertainment, and environmental responsibility. The outdoor living area turns into a sanctuary where campers can relax, connect with nature, and enjoy the small pleasures of outdoor life—whether in an RV, tent or beneath the stars.

CHAPTER V

Connecting with Nature

Hiking Trails and Outdoor Activities

Hiking trails and participating in outdoor activities provide people with a deep connection to nature, offering opportunities for adventure, reflection, and appreciation of the natural world in addition to physical activity. For instance, hiking routes wind through various environments, from tranquil forests to craggy mountains, providing hikers of all skill levels with multiple experiences. Various outdoor activities, such as stargazing, birdwatching, camping, and photography, facilitate a comprehensive interaction with the outdoors. This essay explores the many facets of outdoor activities and hiking paths, including their advantages, disadvantages, and transforming potential for individuals who want to lose themselves in the splendor of nature.

Hiking routes provide entrance points to the vast outdoors, enticing hikers to discover and travel through environments that might not be reachable in other ways. Hiking is a popular sport for people of all ages and fitness levels since it is very accessible, requiring little more than suitable footwear and not much other equipment. Hiking routes range in difficulty from family-friendly strolls to strenuous climbs that try the endurance of seasoned travelers. Every route offers a different experience whole of senses, from the sound of rustling leaves to the aroma of pine or the expansive views that open up with each stride, whether it winds through a verdant forest, climbs a mountain crest, or follows the contours of a shoreline.

Hiking has many mental and emotional benefits in addition to its physical ones. Immersion in nature has been associated with lowered stress levels, happier moods, and increased general wellbeing. Hiking provides a break from the monotonous pace of daily routines, screens, and traffic, enabling people to disconnect from the stresses of modern life. Walking's rhythmic pace and the visual and aural elements of the surrounding scenery combine to produce a meditative atmosphere that promotes calmness and relaxation. A positive outlook and a stronger bond with nature are also fostered by accomplishment and confidence from finishing a problematic trek or reaching a summit.

Hikers can discover a wide variety of environments thanks to the diversity of hiking trails, which reflects the ecological richness of the Earth. Every route offers an intimate experience with the natural world, from desert pathways covered with distinctive flora to coastal trails that meander along immaculate shorelines. A rich diversity of landscapes is available in national parks, wilderness areas, and hiking-only zones, each with unique flora and wildlife. Hiking in these varied settings enables people to observe the complex interactions across ecosystems, which promotes a greater comprehension and admiration of the fragile balance of nature.

Hiking trails are just one type of outdoor activity; there are many more that suit a wide range of hobbies and tastes. Popular outdoor activities such as camping allow people to spend more time in nature than just one day and offer a fully immersing experience outside. Camping provides a feeling of self-sufficiency and a direct connection with the natural world, whether you set up camp in a designated area or a distant wilderness. Camping is a classic outdoor experience because of the distinct atmosphere created by the crackling of a campfire, the peace of a starry night, and the rustling of leaves.

Birdwatching introduces lovers to the fantastic world of avian species and is frequently seen as a peaceful and quiet pastime. With the aid of field guides and binoculars, birdwatchers investigate a variety of habitats, from wetlands and woods to urban parks, to see rare species and study the habits of well-known ones. Observing birds fosters patience, attention, and an acute understanding of the complex patterns seen in their life. The vast array of species adds a dimension of discovery to outdoor activities, each of which is adapted to its own environment and displays unique behaviors that can turn casual onlookers into ardent bird aficionados.

Another way people interact with the outdoors is

through photography, which captures the essence and beauty of natural environments. Outdoor photographers use cameras, lenses, and an artistic eye to capture and preserve fleeting moments, such as the way sunlight plays on a mountain peak, the reflection of a sunset in a serene lake, or the minute details of a flower. The observational component of outdoor activities is enhanced by photography, which motivates people to take in the subtleties of their environment and share the beauty they see with a larger audience. Today, with the popularity of visual storytelling, outdoor photography is a valuable tool for capturing nature's breathtaking vistas and life-changing adventures.

Stargazing is an activity that encourages people to

reflect on the secrets of the cosmos and extends beyond daytime hours. Outside of city lights, stargazers take in the celestial display overhead, recognizing constellations, following astronomical happenings, and taking in the grandeur of space. The best circumstances for viewing celestial phenomena are at dark sky reserves and approved stargazing locations, making for an incredible and humble experience. Stargazing gives outdoor activities a heavenly touch and inspires people to reflect on the secrets of the cosmos and recognize how intertwined Earth is with the larger universe.

Hiking routes and outdoor activities have many advantages, but there are drawbacks and things to consider. Environmental conservation is paramount since increased foot traffic on well-traveled hiking paths can cause habitat disruption, erosion, and the destruction of fragile ecosystems. Minimizing the impact on natural surroundings requires responsible hiking behaviors, such as keeping on authorized paths, honoring wildlife habitats, and following the Leave No Trace philosophy. Similarly, outdoor pursuits like birdwatching and camping call for a careful approach to guarantee that taking pleasure in nature doesn't jeopardize its ecological integrity.

Safety must always come first when going outside, especially in isolated or difficult areas. With the right equipment, enough water, navigational aids, and trail expertise, hikers can be well-prepared. When participating in outdoor activities like camping, outdoor enthusiasts should have the gear they need to stay safe, warm, and dry. Stargazers should know their surroundings and follow safety precautions, especially if they go to distant locations for the best visibility. Being ready and clearly understanding the dangers involved are essential to enjoying outdoor activities in a safe and satisfying manner.

Another thing to consider while promoting the diversity of hiking trails and outdoor activities is accessibility. Not all natural areas are easily accessible, even though many routes are made to suit different fitness levels and skills. To make outdoor activities more inclusive, facilities for people with disabilities must be provided, accessible paths must be built, and awareness of accessible outdoor options must be raised. Ensuring that outdoor activities are accessible to all individuals, irrespective of their physical capabilities, is a crucial measure in cultivating an outdoor community that is more inclusive.

Participation from the community is essential to the preservation of hiking trails and other natural areas. As stewards of these places, local communities frequently seek to preserve trails, carry out conservation projects, and instruct tourists on appropriate outdoor behavior. The sustainability of outdoor activities is enhanced by volunteering in the community, participating in conservation initiatives, and adhering to trail organizations' rules. To ensure that future generations can continue to appreciate the beauty of hiking trails and participate in outdoor activities, a feeling of community promotes a shared responsibility for maintaining the integrity of natural environments.

To sum up, hiking paths and outdoor pursuits give

people access to nature's marvels while also positively affecting their physical, mental, and emotional well-being. Hikers can go across various landscapes, each with unique appeal and difficulties, thanks to the extensive network of hiking paths. Camping, birdwatching, photography, and astronomy are examples of outdoor pursuits that improve the

Outdoor activity encourages a closer relationship with

the natural environment. While issues like accessibility, safety, and environmental preservation need to be addressed, outdoor activities continue to have an unmatched transforming potential. People may continue to discover, enjoy, and be inspired by the immense beauty of hiking trails and the great outdoors via conscientious engagement, community involvement, and a shared commitment to protecting natural spaces.

Wildlife Encounters on the Road

Embarking on a road trip transcends the confines of human exploration, often opening the door to unexpected and enchanting encounters with wildlife. With its many landscapes and ecosystems, the open road offers an opportunity for various animal sightings, from the ordinary to the remarkable. Whether traveling through national parks, across vast plains, or along coastal routes, seeing animals in their native habitats enhances the experience and fosters a sense of connection with the landscape. This paper explores the complex world of roadside wildlife encounters, including species variety, ethical issues surrounding wildlife viewing, and the significant effects these encounters can have on travelers.

The dynamic variety of landscapes that road travel exposes visitors to, each supporting a unique diversity of animals, is one of its special features. National parks are exceptional places to see animals because of their various habitats and conserved ecosystems. From the famous Yellowstone bison herds to the elusive Yosemite mountain lions, these protected sites provide a window into the complex web of life that lives there. Driving along coastal roads offers a chance to see wildlife, like seabirds swooping overhead and whales breaching in the distance. Surprising encounters can be found along seemingly ordinary highway segments, such as animals grazing beside the road or butterflies performing complicated dances in meadows. The road trip's constantly shifting scenery allows wildlife to paint its own story, adding moments of wonder and intimacy to the journey.

Significant mammal encounters are among the most captivating and unforgettable experiences of traveling. Seeing a male elk bugling amid early dawn or a moose walking along a peaceful lakeside road inspires awe for the natural world. Bear sightings in places like the Pacific Northwest or the Rocky Mountains become more than just an observation of animals; they symbolize the wildness that still exists in the continent's center. Viewing these animals from the security of a moving vehicle permits visitors to observe their behavior without upsetting their innate cycles, promoting a spirit of harmony and reverence for the untamed residents of the regions the route winds through.

Road excursions are an excellent way for birdwatchers to see a wide variety of birds since the different settings and ecosystems along the way attract various bird species. The road ride turns into a rolling bird blind, with opportunities for identification and observation of everything from songbirds fluttering through forests to raptors flying over broad plains. While wetlands and marshes throughout the road serve as havens for waterfowl and wading birds, coastal excursions offer sights of seabirds. Birdwatching while driving has a serendipitous quality that enhances the overall diversity of the trip experience by bringing unexpected species into view.

Encounters with marine life along coastal highways and rivers provide a unique dimension to the mosaic of animal sightings while driving. Travelers who drive along coastal roads can see whales in all their majestic majesty, from the famous beach of humpback whales to the sleek silhouette of orcas slicing through the waters. Dolphins diving alongside boats and seals lounging on rocky beaches provide insights into the many marine ecosystems that mirror the terrestrial voyage. Coastal bird colonies give even more allure to the experience of driving down the shore by blending the land and the water with their raucous calls and whirling flocks.

Although seeing wildlife while driving has an undeniable draw, ethical issues are vital to protecting the animals' welfare and preserving their natural activities. Refusing to feed wild animals, keeping a safe distance, and causing as little disturbance as possible to their ecosystems are all essential aspects of responsible wildlife viewing. Using telescopic lens cameras and binoculars, tourists can see animals without disturbing them in their homes. It is crucial to remember that seeing wildlife is a luxury and that courteous, nonintrusive observation of animals in line with ecological stewardship and conservation principles is the aim.

Respecting animals also means keeping vulnerable habitats safe and those living there. Natural spaces can be preserved by following park rules, staying on approved pathways, and honoring habitat limits. Because of the delicate balance between flora and fauna, national parks frequently enforce stringent regulations to protect wildlife populations. Travelers can improve their ethical approach by being familiar with these rules and adopting them into their road trip plans. Road trippers become stewards of the land and actively contribute to conservation initiatives to protect the environments they pass through by reducing the influence of humans on ecosystems.

The cornerstone of appropriate animal encounters on the road is education and awareness. One encounter can deepen one's appreciation for these beings and strengthen one's bond with the natural world by gaining knowledge about the ecological roles, habits, and habitats of the animals. Educational programs, ranger-led tours, and informational materials that offer insights into the local ecosystems and the creatures that inhabit them are available in many national parks and wildlife reserves. To broaden their understanding and help others react more sensibly and responsibly when they come across wildlife while driving, travelers can also use field guides, applications for identifying animals, and internet resources.

Roadside wildlife encounters have a profoundly transforming effect on travelers that goes beyond the initial joy of observation. Spending time with animals can make people feel humble and rooted in understanding their role in the larger scheme of things. Beyond simple observation, the delicate dance of a fox hunting for prey or the group chatter of a prairie dog colony beckons visitors to join in on the more remarkable story of life as it plays out in the wild. These interactions can kindle a love for conservation and inspire people to fight to preserve natural areas and the animals that live there.

Photography becomes a moving medium for preserving and remembering the pleasure of roadside wildlife encounters. In addition to being tangible keepsakes, photographs highlight the natural world's diversity, fragility, and beauty. Using long lenses, paying attention to animal cues, and not disrupting nesting sites are ethical photography techniques that allow tourists to capture their experiences without endangering the subjects' well-being. Travelers can share their experiences and encourage others to value and preserve the beauty of nature by using the photos they take of wildlife encounters to create a visual narrative.

In summary, they are seeing wildlife while traveling

creates a unique and remarkable experience by bringing wonder, a sense of connection, and a deep respect for the natural world into the travelogue. Every experience enhances the depth of the road trip story, from the majestic presence of massive beasts to the delicate flutter of butterflies. Ethically sound methods of watching wildlife guarantee that these interactions are sustainable and support the preservation of ecosystems. These experiences have a lasting impact beyond the length of the road trip, teaching people valuable lessons and transforming them into lifelong admirers of the richness and beauty of wildlife and their habitats.

Maximizing the RV Experience in Nature's Playground

The world of recreational vehicle travel is a perfect symphony of the wide road and nature's embrace. The recreational vehicle, also known as an RV, is more than just a means of transportation; it's a doorway to an unforgettable and immersive outdoor experience. RV fans may make the most of their time in nature's playground, whether traveling along breathtaking highways, camping in national parks, or pitching their tent by a peaceful lakeside. This essay delves into the various dimensions of optimizing the RV experience, encompassing the liberty of movement and adaptability of camping spots, as well as the significance of eco-friendliness and the deep bond with the environment that RV travel enables.

The mobility an RV provides is fundamental tc the experience. RV aficionados have more freedom to choose their route when traveling than those who follow set schedules and hotel reservations. Travelers can veer off course to discover a hidden gem or spend more time in a breathtaking location, turning the open road into a canvas on which they can paint their adventure. The feeling of independence goes beyond the freeways, enabling RVers to explore remote locations that might not be reachable by other modes of transportation and go off the well-traveled route. Whether driving through seaside towns, over mountain passes, or across deserts, an RV trip makes the travel itself an essential component of the adventure.

One of the best things about RVing is that you can choose your camping spots, which gives you an unmatched sense of independence and connection to the natural world. Campgrounds and RV parks provide a range of choices, from fully equipped campsites to more rustic settings that accommodate different tastes. With their specially designed campgrounds for RVs, national parks transform into unspoiled havens where visitors can wake up to birdsong and leaves rustling. While desert areas offer an arresting and dramatic backdrop for RV camping, lakeside parks give peace with views of the surrounding water. Choosing a campsite near hiking trails, picturesque vistas, or animal habitats adds to the whole experience and smoothly combines the RV way of life with the beauties of nature.

Sustainability, which emphasizes responsible behaviors that reduce the environmental impact of travel, emerges as a crucial factor in optimizing the RV experience. RV travelers are urged to travel carefully through their environments by adopting the Leave No Trace philosophy as a guiding concept. Eco-friendly features in modern RVs include water-saving systems, solar power alternatives, and energy-efficient appliances. By implementing conscientious habits like cutting back on trash, reusing goods, and using fewer single-use plastics, RVers may further support sustainability. Selecting parks that highly value environmental preservation and follow eco-friendly programs guarantees that the RV experience aligns with ecological stewardship concepts.

Beyond the traditional lines between interior and outdoor living, a key component of optimizing the RV experience is developing a deep relationship with nature. RVs are made to be cozy and independent living spaces, but they are unique in how well they blend in with the surroundings. Vast panoramas of landscapes are seen through large windows, bringing the outside inside. Awning-covered outside spaces transform into an RV extension, forming a transitional area where travelers can eat, unwind in the shade, or take in the beauty of the environment. RV travel allows visitors to immerse themselves fully in the vast outdoors' sights, sounds, and smells, fostering a close relationship with nature.

The RV experience sparks a more deliberate and aware approach to traveling. Traveling in an RV provides a break from the hectic pace of modern life. It allows you to take it leisurely, enjoy the ride, and enjoy the scenery. The ease of living in an RV promotes a minimalist approach, encouraging visitors to place more value on experiences than material belongings. Hiking, fishing, and stargazing are outdoor pursuits essential to the RV lifestyle and provide chances for physical activity and a closer relationship with the environment. Traveling in an RV encourages people to adopt a more thoughtful and aware approach to world travel, cultivating appreciation for the scenery and natural environments.

Aside from making the most of the RV experience, it's essential to embrace the community of like-minded people passionate about travel, adventure, and the great outdoors—the RV community is diverse and hospitable. Campsites and RV parks act as social hubs where other travelers congregate to exchange experiences, advice, and tales. Beyond the actual campsites, there is a sense of community because social media organizations, online forums, and RV clubs bring together travelers worldwide. The RV lifestyle turns into a shared adventure where experienced travelers mentor beginners and provide a global feeling of community. The RV community's camaraderie improves the whole experience by creating bonds and friendships long after the road trip ends.

To get the most out of your RV trip, you must oe flexible and self-sufficient, especially when traveling to isolated or less-visited locations. Travelers in RVs get experience navigating obstacles, including shifting weather patterns, unforeseen detours, and the odd mechanical problem. People living in RVs develop a problem-solving mindset and become skilled at troubleshooting and creating creative solutions. A basic understanding of RV maintenance, such as tire care, fluid checks, and minor repairs, gives travelers the confidence to hancle problems while on the road, enhancing the adventure's sense of independence. Traveling in an RV fosters flexibility, an important life skill that leads to a more resourceful and adaptable approach to many facets of daily living.

The voyage of an RV trip is dynamic, with new encounters, discoveries, and landscapes to be found every day. Journeyers acquire the skill of valuing the ups and downs of the journey, accepting the uncertainty and delights that await them at every bend. RV travel's cadence becomes a metaphor for life in general, where the trip is just as important as the final destination. The kind of thinking that is developed on the road—a combination of openness, curiosity, and grat'tude for the moment—is not limited to The RV lifestyle impacts how people face difficulties, recognize accomplishments, and interact with their surroundings.

To sum up, making the most of your RV experience in nature's playground involves various factors, including your freedom of movement, the flexibility of your camping options, the significance of sustainability, and your deep connection to the natural world. The RV lifestyle is more than just a method of traveling; it's a way of living intentionally, gratefully, and with a profound respect for the world's natural beauties. RV aficionados discover the full potential of the RV experience by hitting the open road, connecting with other travelers, and developing a lasting passion for the diversity and beauty of nature. They also get to enjoy the richness of landscapes.

CHAPTER VI

Savoring Local Flavors

Exploring Regional Cuisine on the Road

Embarking on a road trip transcends the mere act of traversing distances; it is a journey that unfolds along the contours of landscapes, cultures, and, perhaps most deliciously, regional cuisines—traveling and discovering a place's culinary heritage while on the road is a sensory feast that introduces you to the many tastes, textures, and preparation methods that make each place unique. Regional cuisine becomes a crucial component of the road trip experience, with options ranging from food trucks and roadside cafes to small restaurants hidden in picturesque towns. This essay explores the delicious and diverse world of traveling and sampling local cuisine, revealing the distinctive culinary experiences awaiting visitors and the cultural stories infused into each bite.

Anticipating local specialties that capture the spirit of a location is one of the intrinsic pleasures of traveling and sampling native food. Every location takes pride in its unique culinary offerings, influenced by the local topography, history, and cultural legacy. Travelers can find hidden jewels and landmark establishments by following suggestions from locals and roadside signs, which serve as culinary compasses. Pursuing local food turns a road trip into a gastronomic journey, with each meal acting as a pass to the tastes and histories of the places visited. Delicious street food in busy markets, seafood along coastal roads, and BBQ in the American South—regional cuisine becomes a colorful thread woven into the fabric of the travel experience.

Regional cuisine's varied and eclectic character is influenced by the melting pot of cultures that characterizes various regions. For instance, the enormous size of the United States translates into a gastronomic mosaic where every state, city, and town offers a distinct culinary character. Soulful foods like gumbo, jambalaya, and fried chicken are abundant in the Southern states, where Creole, Cajun, and traditional Southern cuisines influence them. Tacos, enchiladas, and chili are among the most popular dishes in the Southwest, thanks to the influence of Mexican cooking customs. While the Midwest celebrates robust meals like deep-dish pizza and Chicago-style hot dogs, the Pacific Northwest celebrates the abundance of the sea with fresh seafood. Travelers can experience a cross-cultural gastronomic trip by exploring regional cuisine and tasting the various influences that have influenced a region's culinary environment.

The road trip diner is a legendary institution for discovering regional cuisine, a nostalgic and casual atmosphere where travelers can enjoy traditional comfort meals. With their vinyl booths, chrome trimmings, and extensive menus, diners' diners become time capsules that take them back in time. Whether they're enjoying a homemade pie, a juicy burger, and fries, or a big breakfast of pancakes and bacon, diners perfectly capture the essence of the American road trip dining experience. In addition to serving delicious food, restaurants act as community centers where locals and visitors congregate to exchange tales and suggestions that enhance the experience of taking a road trip.

When it comes to investigating local food, food trucks are becoming more and more vivid and active, especially in urban and festival settings. These mobile kitchens provide a variety of international and regional flavors while traveling through parks, city streets, and festivals. Gourmet burgers and handcrafted tacos, as well as unique fusion meals, are all perfectly embodied by food trucks. Food trucks' accessibility and informality encourage tourists to go on spontaneous food adventures to sample various dishes in a relaxed and friendly setting. Traveling to explore local cuisine on the go takes on a new and innovative dimension thanks to food trucks' diverse and constantly changing offerings.

The allure of regional cuisine encompasses sit-down eateries and the genuineness of nearby markets and culinary celebrations. Farmers' markets become hubs of local flavors, with their stalls piled high with handmade goods, artisanal goods, and fresh fruit. They are trying out locally produced preserves, enjoying fruits from the farm, and sampling handcrafted cheeses, all linked directly to the region's abundant agricultural produce. Food festivals transport visitors to a sensory extravaganza of flavors, scents, and live cultural acts while honoring particular foods or culinary customs. Enjoying a seafood festival in New England, a chili cook-off in Texas, or a garlic festival in California—these gatherings highlight a region's culinary character in a fun and social environment.

Drinks from the region, such as unique cocktails, artisan beers, and wines, provide visitors with a taste of the essence of the place while they explore the local food. Because of their innovative and handcrafted methods of brewing beer, craft breweries have grown to be essential to the character of many localities. The iconic vineyards of Napa Valley, the bourbon distilleries of Kentucky, and the craft beer movement in the Pacific Northwest all represent the regional beverage culture. Local cocktails offer a liquid history of the area's history and cultural influences because they frequently use local flavors and ingredients. Travelers can toast to the unique flavors of the road by sampling a local beer, wine, or cocktail as a lovely compliment to exploring local food.

A road trip's gastronomic diversity reflects the many climates and topographies influencing each location. Because they are close to the ocean, coastal areas have a plethora of seafood, ranging from tasty shrimp on the Gulf Coast to exquisite lobster in Maine. Hearty cuisine is served in inland places; in the Southern states, barbecue is the delectable specialty, and farm-to-table cuisine is thriving in agricultural districts. Unique products, including wild berries, game meats, and handmade cheeses, are grown in mountainous terrain. Traveling by car transforms into a gastronomic adventure that reflects the topography and climate of the region, allowing guests to enjoy the flavors that result from the fusion of topography, climate, and culinary heritage.

While traveling, regional food can provide access to the histories and cultural narratives of the places you visit. Recipes passed down through the decades tell the tales of the people who live in a place—their hardships, victories, and festivals. Discovering regional cuisine entails investigating the cultural background that gives each dish its significance and enjoying the flavors. Native American ingredients, recipes, and cooking methods

Techniques provide information about a place's history and identity. Each meal has the resonance of history and tradition because local chefs and culinary artists become storytellers who preserve and evolve the culinary legacy of their communities.

Traveling and sampling local food inspires a spirit of culinary adventure and a readiness to venture beyond one's comfort zone. Tasting local specialties that are new or unusual can be an adventure in and of itself, broadening one's palate and introducing one to unique culinary delights. The road trip turns into a voyage of gastronomic exploration, whether you indulge in regional specialties made with uncommon ingredients, try out exotic cuisine in ethnic areas, or take part in culinary challenges. Every meal becomes a gastronomic adventure when one is open to embracing the unexpected and is directed by the advice of locals and the charm of authenticity.

Traveling to discover local food not only satisfies the senses and the palate but can also make a lasting impression on the communities in which it is experienced. Supporting neighborhood eateries, farmers, and food producers is one way to help the places you visit maintain their economic viability. Locating independently run businesses, farm-to-table eateries, and family-run businesses guarantees that the road trip experience becomes a mutually beneficial exchange that benefits both the tourists and the communities they visit. Positive culinary experiences are best shared by word-of-mouth, social media, or online reviews, which increases the success and visibility of nearby businesses and promotes a sense of support and community among them.

To sum up, traveling and sampling local food is a sensory and cultural experience that turns eating into a pleasurable and absorbing activity. From food trucks and eateries to farmers' markets and food festivals, each location along the route offers a chance to experience the unique tastes and local history. Travelers are given an insight into the histories, customs, and identities of the places they visit through the gastronomic diversity encountered, which reflects the geographical and cultural fabric of the region. A road trip turns into a gastronomic adventure through regional cuisine with every bite, celebrating the diverse and savory world that lies ahead for those who are open to exploring it.

Farmers' Markets and Local Food Experiences

Farmers' markets stand as vibrant intersections where the agricultural roots of communities intertwine with the culinary aspirations of residents and adventurous travelers alike. These dynamic markets, either found strewn across vast fields or tucked away in the center of towns and cities, are more than just locations to purchase fresh fruit; they are centers of regional culture, a celebration of sustainability, and the agricultural fabric that unites a region. Experiencing your way through stalls filled with produce, handmade goods, fruits, and vegetables makes farmers' markets unique. This essay delves into the complex world of farmers' markets and local food experiences, illuminating these venues' role in strengthening ties within communities, promoting regional agriculture, and offering a taste experience of a place's flavors.

The direct interaction between customers and regional producers is the essence of the farmers' market experience. In contrast to the impersonal exchanges that frequently define grocery shopping, farmers' markets offer a chance for direct communication with the people who grow the produce that is on display. Producers of food, crafts, and agriculture take on the role of storytellers, narrating the histories of their goods and the time, effort, and love put into growing or making them. Customers can ask questions regarding farming practices, production processes, and the sources of the items they buy because this direct engagement promotes transparency and confidence. Producer-consumer interaction goes beyond simple business to become a shared experience, a chance to build relationships and learn about the nuances of regional farming.

The seasonality of farmers' markets enhances the dynamic and always-evolving nature of local food experiences. The products at the market change as the year goes on to mirror the natural cycles of abundance and scarcity. Bright displays of early harvest crops, strawberries, and tender greens are brought forth by spring—summer's harvest bursts in many vibrant fruits, tomatoes, and herbs. Winter brings a variety of robust greens, citrus fruits, and preserved foods, while autumn gives a tapestry of pumpkins, apples, and root vegetables. Because the market is cyclical, it follows the natural rhythm of the area, encouraging customers to value the unique harvest of each season and the short shelf life of particular items. Visiting farmers' markets offers a unique window into the local terroir, and it turns into a culinary trip that unfolds with the seasons.

Farmers' markets are recognized for their sustainability, encompassing ecological responsibility, decreased carbon emissions, and preservation of regional ecosystems. These markets' direct-to-consumer business strategy does away with the necessity for the substantial packaging, refrigeration, and transportation of traditional supply chains. Customers can mitigate greenhouse gas emissions through local product purchasing and endorse environmentally conscious agriculture practices. Additionally, many farmers' markets support organic and regenerative agricultural techniques, pushing farmers to embrace ways that improve soil fertility, biodiversity, and water conservation. Sustainable agriculture preserves the agricultural legacy that gives a place its identity while also helping the environment and local food systems remain viable over the long term.

Farmers' markets offer a wide variety of homemade delights, artisanal goods, and fresh produce. These markets bring together local cheese makers, bakers, and other culinary entrepreneurs, who provide a wealth of goods that highlight the inventiveness and skill of the neighborhood. Authentic cheeses, recently baked bread, handcrafted chocolates, and distinctive jams are essential for the farmers' market encounter. These artisanal offerings enhance The local culinary experience, allowing customers to discover the subtleties of handcrafted and small-batch goods. The market becomes a platform for gastronomic discovery, with each handmade dish telling a tale of invention, tradition, and dedication to excellence.

The experience of visiting the farmers' market goes beyond simple shopping and instead becomes a place for neighbors, friends, and families to come together, celebrate, and build relationships. The vibrant environment of farmers' markets fosters a sense of community, interspersed with live music, laughter, and conversation. Both locals and guests congregate to swap recipes, tell tales, and celebrate the shared experience of promoting regional farmers. Farmers' markets frequently act as hubs for cultural festivities, educational seminars, and community events that foster a feeling of community and shared identity. The market square is a microcosm of the neighborhood, where people interact, and a shared commitment to sustainability and neighborhood resilience is strengthened.

Tasting and enjoying regional cuisines is part of the sensory experience farmers' markets offer. Many markets have food sellers and stalls with ready-to-eat meals that highlight the variety of local cuisine. Farmers' markets offer diverse food options, from artisanal ice cream and freshly squeezed juices to gourmet sandwiches and ethnic meals, which mirror the ever-changing and varied local food scenes. Guests can go on a culinary journey, tasting dishes that are influenced by regional culinary traditions and produced using locally sourced ingredients. Chefs and food entrepreneurs can experiment, invent, and spread their love of regional cuisines to a broader audience by using the market as a canvas.

Additionally, farmers' markets are essential for developing a greater awareness of our food sources and advancing food literacy. At these markets, educational programs, cooking demos, and workshops frequently take center stage, educating customers about the nutritional advantages of locally produced produce, seasonal eating, and cooking techniques. Farmers become instructors, imparting knowledge about the difficulties and benefits of sustainable farming. Visitors of all ages can learn about the complexities of agriculture, the value of biodiversity, and the effects of food choices on both environmental and human well-being in this classroom-like setting. Through interacting with regional farmers and taking part in educational initiatives, consumers become more aware of the significance of local food systems and their influence on

Farmers' markets provide a concrete and significant means for consumers to support local agriculture and strengthen the economic stability of their communities. Local farmers, artists, and small companies gain directly from the financial exchanges at these markets, establishing a circle of economic sustainability. Customers can help preserve the cultural legacy and customs ingrained in area agriculture by buying directly from local growers. The economic impact spreads throughout the neighborhood, sustaining family farms' continuous viability, encouraging entrepreneurship, and providing jobs. Farmers' markets develop into vital financial hubs, enabling nearby communities to control their food environments and preserve their linkages to the land.

Farmers' markets are returning in both urban and rural areas, indicating a more significant cultural movement towards a more deliberate and mindful attitude to food consumption. Customers are looking for alternatives to industrialized, mass-produced food systems more and more because they understand how important it is to support local businesses and value having a relationship with the people who grow their food. Farmers' markets provide an alternative model for prioritizing openness, sustainability, and community involvement. They embodied the ideals of ethical consumption. A decision to support local resilience, preserve agricultural diversity, and participate in a more just and sustainable food system is made when one shops at a farmers' market.

To sum up, farmers' markets and local food experiences help to support local economies, build community ties, and provide a taste experience of a region's cuisines. They also capture the richness and diversity of regional agriculture. Rather than being merely transactional places to buy groceries, these lively marketplaces have developed into cultural centers that honor their surrounding areas' customs, histories, and culinary diversity. The farmers' market experience transforms into a celebration of sustainability, community, and the shared journey towards a more mindful and connected approach to food as customers and producers unite at the market square crossroads.

Cooking Tips and RV-Friendly Recipes

RV travel carries the challenge and delight of cooking in a transportable and tiny space, which is a part of the culinary adventure that RV travel delivers. Learning how to cook in a recreational vehicle (RV) is not only a practical necessity for people living a nomadic lifestyle, but it also presents an opportunity to enhance the trip experience by preparing delectable meals at home. This essay will discuss cooking methods and recipes suitable for RVs. We will also uncover the strategies that can be utilized to create delicious dishes while navigating the limits of limited space, resources, and different kitchen setting configurations. The purpose of this investigation is to educate RV enthusiasts with the knowledge and inspiration they need to transform the meals that they prepare while on the move into unforgettable dining experiences. This includes critical kitchen equipment as well as inventive recipes that are adapted for RV kitchens.

A careful selection of kitchen equipment that is both versatile and small is essential to the success of cooking in a recreational vehicle (RV). Because of the limited space in an RV kitchen, every piece of cookware and utensil is essential to the cooking process. It is possible to maximize utility while limiting the amount of storage space required by selecting products with many functions, such as a cast-iron pan that can be used for grilling, baking, and sautéing. Space-saving cookware sets, nested bowls, and collapsible measuring cups and spoons are essential in keeping order and efficiency. Additional cooking alternatives can be obtained using compact kitchen appliances such as a toaster oven or a portable induction cooktop. These products do not take up precious counter space. It is possible to ensure that the kitchen in the RV is prepared for a wide variety of culinary undertakings by investing in kitchen basics that are good quality, stackable, and lightweight.

When it comes to cooking in an RV, strategic meal preparation is an essential component that enables travelers to make the most of the ingredients and resources that are conveniently available to them. Before embarking on a trip, it is beneficial to devise a versatile meal plan that considers the length of the journey, the individual's dietary preferences, and the products available in the area. This will make it easier to go grocery shopping and reduce the amount of food that is wasted. Adopting a modular approach to meal components, such as the preparation of adaptable proteins, cereals, and sauces, enables the freedom to mix and match items to create a variety of unique and fulfilling meals. However, regardless of the availability of food stores along the route, a well-stocked kitchen can be ensured by including pantry items that are shelf-stable and long-lasting. These pantry items include canned goods, dried grains, and spices.

The recipes suitable for use in RVs are developed with the specific limitations of mobile kitchens in mind, emphasizing simplicity, efficiency, and the production of delectable results. One-pot dishes, including casseroles, stews, and stir-fries prepared in a skillet, simplify the cooking process while reducing the amount of cleanup required. Using foil packet recipes, in which the ingredients are tightly wrapped in aluminum foil and then cooked over an open flame or in the oven, provides a cooking method that is both mess-free and very customizable. A dish's flavors are enhanced and a hint of smokiness is added when it is grilled, regardless of whether it is done on an RV stove or an outside grill. Batch cooking, which involves creating a dish in large quantities and then portioning it out for later consumption, is an efficient way to maximize the use of time and resources. It also provides ready-made meals for those days when you are on the road and need a more practical culinary solution.

When it comes to the success of cooking on the go, one of the most essential ingredients is creativity in adapting recipes to the kitchen of an RV. RV chefs can overcome such constraints by embracing the diversity of food and being open to replacements. The use of tortillas as a foundation for pizzas, tacos, or wraps, for example, avoids the requirement for a conventional oven and uses the limited space available for cooking in an RV. Similarly, seeking out recipes for desserts that do not require baking, such as energy bites or refrigerator cakes, can satisfy the desire for sweets without relying on conventional baking techniques. The RV kitchen may be transformed into a dynamic culinary area by allowing for flexibility in the execution of recipes and a desire to experiment with different flavors and techniques. This combination allows the joy of cooking to take precedence over the RV's size and mobility constraints.

Improving the efficiency of food preparation requires making the most of both time and resources, which is a significant factor while working in the mobile environment of an RV kitchen. It is possible to expedite the cooking process and reduce the counter space required by preparing the materials in advance. Examples include cutting vegetables, marinating proteins, and putting together meal kits. By embracing pre-cooked or pre-packaged foods, such as rotisserie chicken or pre-cut vegetables, one can reduce the time spent in the kitchen and speed up the cooking process. Additionally, keeping a kitchen space that is well-organized and clear of clutter is an effective way to improve efficiency. This allows chefs to concentrate on the pleasure of cooking rather than struggling with chaotic conditions.

The ability to cook meals outside broadens the culinary repertoire of RV enthusiasts and allows them to relish meals while being surrounded by the natural beauty that is all around them. Grilling, whether on a grill placed on an RV, a portable barbecue, or outside over an open campfire, imparts a delightfully smoky and charred flavor to the prepared food. Using a cast-iron Dutch oven or grill grate, campfire cooking may change the RV camping experience into a new and exciting culinary journey. The perfume of wood smoke infuses each bite with a flavor reminiscent of the countryside. By embracing the relationship between food, nature, and the open road, outdoor cooking not only adds variety to the menu but also improves the whole travel experience, making the RV more enjoyable.

By adopting the practice of mindful cooking, one can cultivate a more profound appreciation for the gastronomic experience that traveling in an RV can provide. The act of cooking may be transformed into a conscious and pleasurable experience by taking the time to relish the process, which includes everything from selecting ingredients to presenting the food. Because they are designed to be compact while still efficient, RV kitchens inspire chefs to concentrate on the fundamentals, prompting them to engage with each step of the culinary process. The concept of mindful cooking comprises more than just the task of making meals; it also includes a knowledge of the regional cuisines, the local ingredients, and the cultural context that enhances the experience of traveling in an RV. Cooking in a recreational vehicle (RV) can be elevated to a holistic and sensory inquiry level when travelers incorporate mindfulness into their cooking experiences.

When it comes to a recreational vehicle's (RV) kitchen, culinary improvisation becomes a valuable talent that enables cooks to adapt and develop.

To address the difficulties that arise from having limited resources or situations that are unanticipated, to create a resilient and creative attitude to RV cooking, it is essential to be open to experimenting with different flavors, trying out new cooking techniques, and accepting the occasional culinary mishap as a part of the journey. The attitude of improvisation extends to the usage of local foods encountered on the tour. This encourages chefs to add fresh produce, artisanal items, and distinctive flavors to their dishes into their recipes. The kitchen in the recreational vehicle (RV) transforms into a destination for culinary adventure, a place where adaptability and inventiveness are king.

In conclusion, the ability to cook in an RV kitchen's

limited but variable space is a skill that can turn preparing meals into an exciting and entertaining adventure. For travelers to enjoy tasty and handmade meals while on the road, it is necessary to equip the mobile kitchen with needed gear, embrace strategic meal planning, and explore recipes compatible with RVs. The gastronomic experience of RV travel can be elevated by including cooking methods specifically designed for an RV's kitchen, as well as by being willing to adapt and experiment. As RV enthusiasts embark on their trips, armed with culinary inventiveness and the joy of cooking, the RV kitchen transforms into a space where the pleasures of the open road combine with the delights of a meal cooked with care.

CHAPTER VII

Community and Camaraderie

Connecting with Fellow RV Enthusiasts

The allure of RV travel extends beyond the freedom of the open road; it encompasses a vibrant and welcoming community of fellow enthusiasts who share a passion for exploration, adventure, and the nomadic lifestyle. There is a sense of camaraderie, shared experiences, and a network of like-minded folks who understand the joys and hardships of life on wheels that can be gained through connecting with other RV lovers. This may be a transformational component of the RV experience. This essay investigates the significance of establishing relationships with other people who share a passion for recreational vehicles (RVs), digging into the channels via which these connections are formed, the advantages of participating in RV communities, and the significant influence that shared experiences and camaraderie have on the journey as a whole.

In a literal sense, the RV community comprises individuals and families who have decided to travel the less traveled path. This community is diverse and welcoming. A wide range of lives and backgrounds are represented within the recreational vehicle (RV) community. This includes retirees who are interested in taking a leisurely tour of the country. These young families are excited about the prospect of homeschooling and lone travelers seeking independence. One thing that all of these different people have in common is a profound appreciation for the beauty that can be discovered along the highways and in the peaceful corners of the country, as well as a love for the nomadic lifestyle and a yearning for independence. This rich diversity may be tapped into by connecting with people who share a passion for recreational vehicles (RVs), which provides an opportunity to learn from one another, exchange insights, and form friendships that transcend geographical limits.

There are various ways to connect within the RV community, much like the folks themselves. Campgrounds and RV parks serve as natural gathering places for travelers, where they can meet new people, get advice from one another, and even develop friendships on the spur of the moment. To establish a feeling of community and allow folks with similar interests to meet one another, many RV parks offer social events, ranging from potluck dinners to group walks. The scope of the community is further expanded through the use of online forums and social media groups that are specifically dedicated to RV travel. These groups connect enthusiasts from all over the world. Through these virtual places, individuals can share their experiences of the ups and downs of life on the road, seek tips, and exchange advice with one another. Rally events and organized meetings of RV enthusiasts in certain areas provide a more structured setting for community interaction. These events include workshops, lectures, and social activities catering to various interests associated with the RV lifestyle.

When you connect with other people who share your passion for recreational vehicles (RVs), you have the opportunity to engage in social contact and gain access to a wealth of information, helpful advice, and a support network that enhances your RV adventure. Regarding the recreational vehicle (RV) community, firsthand experiences become extremely significant resources. Experienced travelers advise those about to go on their first motorized journey. Creating a collaborative knowledge base that makes the learning curve more accessible for beginners is accomplished through the free sharing of information regarding the navigation of rugged terrains, the optimization of RV settings, and the troubleshooting of common problems. This knowledge-sharing is not limited to technical issues; rather, it encompasses tips on scenic routes, hidden gems, and sites that cannot be missed for whatever reason. The recreational vehicle (RV) community serves as a reservoir of insider information, making every interaction with a fellow enthusiast an opportunity to improve the overall travel experience.

The concept of "boondocking," or dispersed camping, in which RVers opt to camp off-grid in natural settings, is a fascinating example of the sense of community within the world of recreational vehicles (RVs). Regarding boondocking, fans frequently share information on pristine and remote spots, offering others the coordinates and insights necessary to access these hidden jewels. Not only does this culture of sharing and collaboration help preserve natural areas, but it also gives RV travelers the opportunity to explore less traveled and more distinctive paths. The collective dedication of the RV community to enjoy nature's beauties while minimizing their impact on delicate ecosystems is highlighted by the philosophy of responsible boondocking, which is characterized by the values of Leave No Trace and respect for the environment.

A sense of connection and camaraderie that enhances the travel experience is fostered by interacting with other people who share a passion for recreational vehicles (RVs), in addition to the practical benefits. In the way of life that can sometimes be solitary due to the fact that travelers move from one site to another, the connections formed within the RV community become a source of comfort and support. A sense of home can be created on the road through shared campfires, potluck dinners, and group activities. This is a place where people and families can discover company and a sense of purpose that they share. The relationships developed within the RV community frequently go beyond the transient nature of the lifestyle, developing into long-lasting friendships that continue long after the road trip. This sense of belonging becomes an essential component of the RV experience, transforming strangers into traveling companions and fellow enthusiasts into a family that is both extended and supportive.

The recreational vehicle (RV) community is not limited to geographical bounds; borders do not limit it, and it welcomes visitors from all over the world, notwithstanding their location. The community is enriched with diversity and depth thanks to the contributions of international RV enthusiasts drawn to the appeal of experiencing the vast landscapes of North America. Cultural exchanges, language obstacles, and a wide range of travel customs give the connections formed within the RV world a taste reminiscent of the global community. The collective story of the RV community is often enriched by the contributions of international RVers, who frequently bring distinctive points of view, travel experiences, and culinary traditions. As a result of the shared enthusiasm for discovery, a universal language is created, which helps to bridge cultural divides and develop connections that showcase the global appeal of the nomadic lifestyle.

Connecting with other people who have a passion for recreational vehicles (RVs) has a significant impact on the personal development and transformation that individuals and families experience when traveling. Inherently, a recreational vehicle (RV) lifestyle encourages a departure from the familiar, the acceptance of unpredictability, and the cultivation of adaptation. The interaction with a varied group of persons within the RV community enhances this transformative journey. This interaction exposes travelers to various worldviews, lives, and approaches to RV travel. Gaining knowledge from other people transforms into a two-way exchange, where every interaction becomes a chance for personal development and enrichment. The recreational vehicle (RV) community ultimately develops into a dynamic and ever- changing ecosystem, which is formed by the contributions of its members and the collective wisdom gathered from the numerous adventures completed.

People passionate about recreational vehicles (RVs) frequently find inspiration and motivation in the narratives of individuals who have traversed unconventional and one-of-a-kind travels. The blogs, vlogs, and personal narratives that fellow RVers share become a source of support and a window into the numerous ways in which individuals have embraced the nomadic lifestyle. These accounts highlight the variety of experiences that can be had, ranging from sweeping journeys across the country to leisurely explorations of the beauty of the surrounding surroundings. The stories in this collection serve as a source of motivation for aspiring RV travelers, providing them with insights into the problems and victories that are waiting for them along the way. The shared narratives within the RV community create a tapestry of inspiration.
This tapestry weaves together stories of resiliency, discovery, and the transformational power of the nomadic journey.

A further contribution that the recreational vehicle (RV) community makes is to advocate for protecting public lands, responsible outdoor recreation, and environmentally responsible travel habits. Individuals passionate about recreational vehicles (RVs) frequently find themselves at the center of discussions concerning environmental preservation, the ideals of Leave No Trace, and the significance of limiting travel's impact on natural ecosystems. The commitment of the recreational vehicle (RV) community to be good stewards of the landscapes they traverse is highlighted by collective actions such as community clean-up projects, environmental education campaigns, and support for conservation groups. RV enthusiasts contribute to the larger discourse concerning the nature of the intersection between recreational travel and the preservation of the environment by participating in conversations about environmentally responsible travel and sustainable travel.

In conclusion, establishing relationships with other

people who have a passion for recreational vehicles (RVs) is a transforming part of the RV experience. It helps cultivate a feeling of community, the exchange of information, and long-lasting ties beyond the fleeting nature of life on the road. When people and families are navigating the trials and delights of the nomadic lifestyle, the RV community, which is diverse and inclusive, becomes a source of inspiration, friendship, and support for them. The relationships within the RV community strengthen the travel experience, transforming it from a solo journey into a shared voyage of discovery and companionship. These connections can be made in various settings, such as through giving advice on internet forums, forming long-lasting friendships at RV parks, or sitting around a campfire.

Joining RV Clubs and Events

The allure of the open road, the freedom to explore diverse landscapes, and the nomadic lifestyle are the elements that draw individuals and families to the world of RV travel. Beyond the lone traveler or family vacation, however, the RV industry is home to a thriving and friendly community. Getting involved in events and joining RV groups are essential parts of the RV experience, providing enthusiasts with an opportunity to connect with like-minded people passionate about living on the road and exchanging expertise. This essay examines the value of attending events and joining RV clubs. It also looks at the advantages of getting involved in the community, the variety of services provided by RV clubs, and the life-changing effects of attending events that honor the spirit of RV travel.

RV clubs act as social hubs, bringing people who are passionate about traveling on wheels and the nomadic lifestyle. These organizations frequently serve various RVers' interests and demographics, providing areas where full-time RVers, weekend warriors, retirees, and families with young children can all feel included. The commonalities include a love of travel, an interest in taking the less-traveled path, and a dedication to accepting the benefits and drawbacks of living in an RV. By joining a group, RV enthusiasts can meet new people, share experiences, and get guidance from those who have traveled through similar situations. These groups, which may be based on particular RV models, travel preferences, or geographical affinities, form a community within RV travel's broad and varied world.

Becoming a member of an RV club has many advantages over socializing. These online forums function as archives of collective expertise, providing many perspectives, pointers, and helpful guidance for both experienced RVers and novices to the way of life. Online discussion boards, newsletters, and club meetings provide venues for sharing knowledge regarding RV upkeep, travel routes, and the newest advancements in RV technology. Each member of these clubs becomes an essential resource due to the cumulative wisdom inside them, and the firsthand experiences and lessons learned along the way serve as priceless guides for others. The abundance of information shared in RV clubs helps newbies learn the ropes more quickly and confidently by guiding them through the complexities of RV living.

RV clubs frequently plan get-togethers and activities to unite their members in a joint celebration of the nomadic way of life. These get-togethers offer chances for adventure, companionship, and the development of enduring friendships. Rallies can be anything from unstructured get-togethers at RV parks to formal events with seminars, scheduled activities, and social meetings.

The atmosphere of camaraderie that permeates these gatherings creates a shared space where people and families can connect, transforming strangers into friends. Rallies serve as a hub for the various narratives within the RV community and a celebration of the shared experience that unites enthusiasts.

Members of RV clubs are guaranteed to find

communities that share their particular hobbies, travel preferences, or regional affinities thanks to the clubs' many themes. For instance, organizations devoted to specific RV types or models offer areas for owners to interact, exchange maintenance advice, and celebrate their shared love of a particular kind of RV. Some target specific groups of people, such as family-oriented clubs that provide kid-friendly activities or retiree clubs that arrange leisurely trips for seniors relishing their golden years of independence. Regional groups give people who live close together a sense of community by promoting local get-togethers or highlighting the beauty of particular locations. RV lovers can find people who share their unique viewpoints and tastes by choosing from various clubs catering to different hobbies.

Through planned caravans and group travel, RV clubs

frequently foster a sense of community that transcends the virtual to the real world. In a caravan, several RVers travel together according to a prearranged schedule, sharing the experience and bonding over a shared voyage. Group travel experiences, such as cross-country odysseys, destination explorations, or themed caravans based on interests or hobbies, offer a unique opportunity to bond with other RV enthusiasts. Caravans provide the advantages of group safety, cooperative navigation, and the excitement of traveling with companions. These trips forge enduring friendships that bind a network of people who have experienced the highs and lows of life on the open road.

RV clubs frequently encourage their members to give

back to the towns and locations they visit by fostering a spirit of philanthropy and community participation.

Numerous organizations arrange volunteer programs, community service assignments, and philanthropic endeavors that enable RVers to impact the communities they visit positively. The RV community has a collective responsibility to be responsible stewards of the environment and active contributors to the communities they visit. This responsibility is demonstrated by initiatives such as environmental conservation, supporting local charities, and organizing campground clean-ups. The feeling of shared duty gives the RV experience a deeper, more meaningful dimension, turning travel into a mission-driven, community-focused activity. The emergence of social media and internet platforms has increased the number of

RV enthusiasts can interact, exchange stories, and ask for guidance. Online forums, social media groups, and virtual communities devoted to RV travel provide easily accessible venues for people to interact with other like-minded travelers from across the globe. These virtual forums allow people to share recommendations, thoughts, and real-time information, forming a vibrant, international network of RV lovers. Travelers can connect with fellow fans, exchange updates from their travels, and seek guidance on the go even when geographical distances separate them, thanks to the instantaneous nature of online connections. In addition to traditional RV clubs, virtual communities provide a platform for people who might not be able to attend in-person events but still want to be a part of the sense of community that characterizes the RV lifestyle.

Beyond the obvious advantages, becoming a member of an RV club and attending activities can profoundly impact one's personal development, viewpoint, and sense of belonging to the community of RV travelers. People are inspired to embrace the full range of opportunities the nomadic lifestyle offers by the many stories and experiences shared within these networks. Learning about creative RV modifications, finding hidden treasures on the road, or understanding various travel philosophies are examples of how exposure to multiple viewpoints found in RV organizations may spur intellectual and personal development. The RV community develops into a dynamic tale that spans individual travels, with each strand adding to the story.

Being involved in RV groups and events opens up new opportunities for social circle expansion, self-discovery, and boundary development. People are encouraged to explore beyond their comfort zones, try new things, and appreciate the unpredictable nature of the open road by the general attitude of adventure in these towns. Participating in RV activities can lead to a life-changing voyage of self-discovery and exploration, whether caravanning to new places or rallying to meet people and build new friendships. People in these communities feel inspired to follow their hobbies, overcome obstacles, and fully experience the richness of the RV lifestyle because of the shared camaraderie and support.

In summary, joining organizations and attending events is a life-changing experience for RV enthusiasts. It gives them a sense of belonging, a pool of knowledge, and enduring relationships that enhance their travels. These groups, based on shared hobbies, modes of transportation, or geographical ties, develop into centers of friendship where people can meet others who share their interests. A culture of adventure, altruism, and shared duty is fostered throughout these communities through rallies, caravans, and virtual connections. Beyond the obvious advantages, interacting with other RVers leads to self-discovery, personal development, and a greater appreciation for the shared adventure that characterizes the nomadic way of life.

Building Lasting Friendships on the Road

The open road, with its endless horizons and ever-changing landscapes, serves as a pathway to exploration and a conduit for forging lasting friendships. For individuals fully engaged in the nomadic lifestyle of recreational vehicle travel, the journey is about the relationships formed along the route, not simply the destinations. Making lifelong friends while traveling becomes a distinctive part of the RV experience, providing a mosaic of connections across national boundaries and societal divides. This essay delves into the unique dynamics of making relationships when traveling, the advantages of living in a nomadic society, and the life-changing power of shared experiences that unite travelers to examine the fundamental relevance of friendship in RV travel.

Because of its natural feeling of movement, the RV lifestyle offers a unique setting for establishing relationships. Living on the road speeds up social interactions, unlike permanent living, where neighbors may move seldom, and community ties develop slowly. Families and individuals come together naturally in campgrounds, RV parks, and public areas to celebrate the everyday experience of living on wheels. A culture of openness and approachability is fostered by the transient nature of RV travel, where neighbors may change frequently as other enthusiasts come and go—having regular talks with neighbors, exchanging tales around the campfire, and lending a helping hand when required all help to create enduring connections.

The variety among RVers enriches the fabric of friendships forged while traveling. A diverse range of backgrounds, ages, and lifestyles are represented among RV travelers, which fosters a vibrant and welcoming atmosphere for forming social bonds. The RV community comprises people from all walks of life, from families going on educational excursions to lone travelers seeking peace, quiet, and self-discovery. These varied origins serve as the cornerstones of friendships, fostering the development of a community where people exchange knowledge, deepen their perspective of the world, and learn from one another. The relationships formed when traveling are not limited by age, profession, or place of origin; they are based on a shared love of discovery and respect for the nomadic way of life.

RV travel's nomadic lifestyle strongly emphasizes the value of forming ties with other travelers and sharing experiences, even through difficult times. RV lovers share a familiar story that forms the basis of enduring friendships, whether negotiating rough terrain, resolving mechanical issues, or appreciating the beauty of a beautiful route. The spirit of RV friendships is embodied in the camaraderie formed around campfires, potluck meals, and spontaneous get-togethers—connections based on the shared delight of the journey and the immediacy of the present. RV travelers develop a distinct language from their shared experiences, a woven web of memories and stories that form the foundation of their friendships.

Traveling friendships are defined by camaraderie and support for one another that goes beyond conventional ideas of neighborhood ties. Families and individuals may find themselves traveling with like-minded people with similar values, hobbies, and travel habits in the RV world. RV friendships are supportive in that people are willing to help out while setting up campgrounds, give advice on traveling, or offer encouragement while driving. The network of friends made while traveling on the road becomes an invaluable resource that improves the RV experience, whether providing technical assistance, suggesting hidden treasures, or just being a listening ear. People who feel supported by their community are more likely to live in a setting where they are seen as valuable members of a more comprehensive network of relationships.

Technology has further changed the nature of establishing and sustaining RV friendships through social media and online venues. RV enthusiasts can interact, exchange experiences, and seek guidance in these virtual groups, regardless of location. Social media groups, online forums, and specialized apps for RV travel enable people to communicate in real-time, allowing them to reconnect with friends they met while traveling and meet new people who share their interests. The online aspect of RV connections contributes to the community by offering a forum for ongoing conversation, information sharing, and commemorating everyday achievements, even while geographically separated. The convergence of real-world and virtual ties enhances the depth of RV friendships, resulting in a dynamic and networked social environment.

The ever-changing scenery and constant movement of recreational vehicles give friendships forged on the road an air of impermanence. Although this transience would appear incompatible with the concept of enduring relationships, it provides RV friendships with a unique quality: an appreciation of the present moment and an understanding of the transience of some relationships. Families and individuals who travel together appreciate the importance of connection in the present moment. The transience of physical closeness fosters an intentional friendship culture in which people deliberately work to build deep bonds while traveling together. Understanding that friendships might change as travel goes on promotes an open, flexible, and profound appreciation for the relationships formed, no matter how short-lived.

Creating lifelong friendships when traveling goes beyond random meetings at campsites or picturesque route encounters. Rallies, RV groups, and planned gatherings offer structured settings where people can meet other enthusiasts with similar connections or interests. Whether geared toward a specific RV model, traveler demographic, or travel style, joining an RV club can forge more specialized and in-depth friendships. The mutual kinship among these groups develops.

A solid basis for relationships enables people to join together over shared interests, take part in planned events, and carry out more deliberate community development. Club events are designed to encourage longer encounters and provide opportunities for friendships to grow and last.

RV friendships have a transforming effect on the entire travel experience, even outside of the immediate social circle. Collaborative travel is frequently the outcome of shared connections; convoys of RVers plan their routes, visit locations together, and develop a sense of camaraderie while traveling. The delight of joint discovery enriches the trip experience, transforming the voyage into a group adventure where obstacles are overcome cooperatively, and victories are shared. Because RV friendships are collaborative, they foster a sense of security and support among members, enabling them to face the uncertainties of travel knowing they are not traveling alone. The companionship of friends while traveling and the common goal they share transform the RV experience from a lonely endeavor into a rewarding group adventure.

In addition to adding to the depth of friendships within the RV community, diversity promotes learning and personal development. Connecting with people from different backgrounds exposes RVers to various viewpoints, cultures, and lifestyles. RV friendships naturally involve the sharing of customs, the exchange of ideas, and the enjoyment of diversity. Within the RV community, the rich experiences of sharing knowledge weave a cultural tapestry that allows people and families to see the world from the perspective of their fellow travelers. In this situation, RV friendships link people from different origins, promoting respect, curiosity, and humanism.

RV friendships have an impact on people's emotional and mental health as well as the wellbeing of families and individuals traveling. Having friends gives one a sense of connection and community that may be comforting and supportive, especially when dealing with the difficulties of traveling in an RV. Friends on the road become pillars of support, whether they are there to listen in uncertain times, offer helpful assistance when things go wrong, or share a good laugh around the campfire. Friendships made through RV travel create an emotional support system essential to the nomadic lifestyle, offering consolation, inspiration, and a common goal that improves the wellbeing of those who travel.

To sum up, creating enduring friendships while traveling in an RV is a life-changing and essential part of the experience, creating a web of relationships that cut across national boundaries and cultural differences. RV travel's transitory lifestyle quickens social interactions and promotes an approachable and transparent culture. Shared experiences, a feeling of community, and mutual support that transcends conventional ideas of neighborhood ties are characteristics of friendships in RVs. These friendships, whether from fortuitous meetings at campgrounds, deliberate relationships made within RV clubs, or online groups made possible by technology, become essential to the nomadic way of life. The transforming power of RV friendships reaches into the personal development, perspective-expansion, and emotional health of travelers and their families.

CHAPTER VIII

Overcoming Challenges

Navigating Weather and Terrain

Navigating the vast and diverse landscapes of the open road is a hallmark of the RV experience, and it comes with its own set of challenges and considerations. None of these issues is as significant and erratic as the weather. The weather can differ significantly between locations, making RV travelers face a dynamic and ever-changing environment. In addition, the terrain that RVers travel on—which varies from accessible freeways to rugged mountain passes—adds another level of complexity. This section delves into the intricacies of weather and terrain navigation in the context of recreational vehicle travel. It looks at how weather patterns affect driving conditions, how travelers deal with weather-related issues, and how to navigate a variety of terrains safely and enjoyably.

The weather, a dynamic and frequently unpredictable force, significantly influences how an RV travels. RV travelers must deal with various weather conditions, from the sun-drenched deserts of the Southwest to the snow-covered landscapes of the northern regions. Understanding the climatic trends of the areas one intends to travel through is the first step toward successfully navigating the weather. Seasonal changes can significantly impact road conditions and the entire travel experience. Examples of these fluctuations include summer heatwaves, winter storms, and the erratic character of spring weather. For RVers, keeping an eye on short- and long-term weather forecasts is essential since it helps them plan routes, make educated judgments, and modify their plans in response to weather-related events.

Proactive planning is crucial in areas vulnerable to extreme weather events like hurricanes, tornadoes, or wildfires. To be informed of evolving circumstances, RV travelers frequently rely on online resources, apps for tracking the weather, and communication with local authorities. Flexible travel planners can react to severe weather warnings by changing their routes or delaying their trips, which makes them valuable assets. Nomads are very adaptive to shifting circumstances and frequently view unpredictable weather as a necessary component of the experience.

Weather affects RV travel in more ways than just safety; it also affects how much fun you have on the trip. Rain showers have the potential to transform dusty roads into muddy obstacles, while strong gusts can increase driving difficulty and compromise the stability of more oversized recreational vehicles. But bad weather doesn't have to dent the spirit of adventure. The well-appointed interiors of RVs provide many with comfort and serenity, making rainy days ideal for cozy inside pursuits like gaming, reading, or just taking in the sound of raindrops hitting the roof. RV travelers who embrace the ebb and flow of weather patterns develop a mindset that improves their resilience and adaptability.

When traveling through inclement weather, the RV's preparation becomes an essential part of the trip. Frequent maintenance checks guarantee that the car is in top shape to tackle various weather conditions, especially before a long journey. This includes ensuring that all vital systems—such as the heating, cooling, and electrical—function effectively, checking the brakes, and ensuring the tires have enough tread. An additional preparation layer is added using weather-appropriate equipment, such as tire chains for winter travel or awnings for shade in hot areas. Additionally, having a fully equipped emergency kit on the road with necessities like tools, communication devices, and first aid supplies offers a safety net in case unanticipated weather conditions materialize.

For RV travelers, snow and ice pose distinct difficulties, requiring extra safety measures and specialized gear. Winterizing the RV is essential for anyone traveling through snowy areas to protect water systems from below-freezing temperatures. Snow chains could be required for traction on snowy roads, and antifreeze treatments shield plumbing systems from harm. Furthermore, to guarantee access to electricity-powered heating systems during the winter, RVers frequently prefer locations with electrical hookups. RVers who travel in cold climates need to strike a balance between adventure and safety, and they also need to arm themselves with the information and resources required to traverse winter terrain with assurance.

On the other hand, high heat presents unique difficulties for RVers. The effectiveness of cooling systems becomes critical in extreme heat. RVers frequently rely on air conditioners, awnings, and well-placed parking in shaded spots to beat the heat. Travelers exposed to intense sunlight must drink enough water and take precautions like wearing clothes that fit correctly and using sunscreen. To lessen the effects of the heat, RVers often choose campsites near coasts or at higher elevations during the sweltering summer months.

The terrain of RV travel varies greatly, much like the weather. RVers travel on various terrains, from wide highways to narrow mountain roads, which require flexibility and cautious navigation. The route chosen becomes even more critical since some RVs may find specific terrain more difficult. For example, larger trailers and RVs could have trouble negotiating tight turns on twisting roads or via tiny mountain passes. RVers frequently use navigation apps explicitly made for traveling in RVs. These apps consider factors like vehicle weight, size, and height limitations to offer routes appropriate for different RVs.

Despite the spectacular sights it offers, RV travelers need help traveling across mountainous terrain. Expertise and attention are required when navigating hairpin turns, tight roads, and steep ascents and descents. When driving in the mountains, RVers frequently take it slow and steady, using lower gears on descents to manage speed and lessen brake strain. On downhill sections, brake temperatures can rise quickly. Careful driving helps avoid brake fade, a condition when the brakes lose their efficacy because they are overheated. Regular maintenance inspections of the braking system are also necessary to guarantee peak performance in hilly areas.

Elevation variations in hilly or mountainous areas can impact the RV's functionality and the health of its inhabitants. Problems associated with altitude, such as reduced oxygen and thinner air, might affect the vehicle's engine performance and the passengers' comfort. RVers adjust to elevation changes gradually, which gives the car and its occupants time to become used to it. Staying adequately hydrated and ventilated becomes essential, and travelers may decide to stay longer at intermediate levels before climbing higher mountain passes.

RV travelers face unique difficulties when traveling through desert environments because of its vast expanses and distinctive attractiveness. Extreme weather necessitates cautious planning and preparation, particularly in the summer. A desert environment requires effective cooling systems, enough water sources, and shade structures. In addition, soft sand or gravel may be present on desert roads; this means that good tire inflation and cautious driving are necessary to prevent getting stuck. Dust storms, frequent in desert areas, can make driving conditions dangerous and impair visibility. RVers frequently monitor weather forecasts and take the appropriate safety measures, like locking up outdoor items and keeping track of any possible storm activity.

RVers should consider the unique attractions and factors of traveling along the coast. The corrosive effects of salt air on RV exteriors offset the attractiveness of beachside camping and ocean vistas. Regular maintenance checks—including rust and corrosion inspections—help prolong the vehicle's lifespan in coastal environments. Additionally, when parking close to the shoreline, consider tides and shifting beach conditions. RVers need to be aware of the accessibility of their chosen beachfront sites, high tide lines, and possible flooding.

Urban settings pose particular difficulties for RV travelers because of the heavy traffic and limited parking. Finding appropriate parking, navigating tight spaces, and navigating metropolitan streets can be difficult jobs. RVers frequently schedule their

Routes to avoid rush hour, use navigation applications that consider routes suitable for RVs through cities and do a prior study on the locations of RV parking. When traveling through urban areas, one must be especially mindful of local traffic laws and restrictions, as some may restrict the kinds and sizes of permitted cars.

The choice of campsites is also influenced by terrain.

Campsites that suit their interests in terms of outdoor activities, natural beauty, and accessibility to attractions are frequently sought after by RVers. RV enthusiasts often choose national and state parks because of their varied scenery and recreational options. However, some parks could restrict the size of RVs, and reservations are frequently required, particularly during the busiest times of the year. To meet the various demands of RV travelers, private RV parks and campgrounds provide multiple services, such as Wi-Fi access and complete hookups. For those looking for seclusion and a connection to nature, boondocking or dispersed camping on public lands offers a more wild and unplugged experience.

In summary, negotiating weather and terrain is a fundamental part of traveling in an RV and calls for a trifecta of readiness, flexibility, and meticulous planning. Weather affects driving and necessitates a proactive approach to comfort and safety, from intense heat to winter storms. RVers successfully manage a variety of weather patterns by utilizing technology, tools for monitoring the weather, and flexible travel schedules. Similarly, different road conditions—from deserts and mountains to coastal areas and urban settings—call for other driving and camping strategies. RVers welcome the difficulties posed by the weather and the terrain, seeing them as essential components of the exciting and enlightening journey that characterizes life on the road rather than as barriers to overcome. As they travel through the always-shifting landscapes, RV enthusiasts exhibit their adaptability and resilience, weaving each trip into a mosaic of experiences that honor the diversity and beauty of their environment.

Handling RV Repairs and Maintenance on the Go

RV travel is a nomadic lifestyle that brings a sense of freedom and discovery, but it also comes with the duty of handling repairs and maintenance while a person is on the move. People who live in recreational vehicles (RVs) become experts in their mobile domain, not only in navigating the open road but also in safeguarding the health and functionality of their rolling homes. This essay dives into the complexities of managing RV repairs and maintenance while on the move. It examines the typical difficulties that RV enthusiasts encounter, the significance of taking a preventative approach to maintenance, and the inventiveness required to troubleshoot and address issues while traveling.

The recreational vehicle (RV), a multi-functional dwelling on wheels, is susceptible to wear and tear as it travels across various terrains and climates. Mechanical systems, electrical components, plumbing, and the general structural integrity of the recreational vehicle (RV) are all subject to hazards on the road. For this reason, RVers need to have a fundamental grasp of the vehicle's systems and techniques for performing routine maintenance. Proactivity is the cornerstone of successful RV ownership. Resolving possible problems before they become more serious is cost-effective and essential for ensuring that a trip experience is safe and pleasurable.

To protect against unanticipated breakdowns while driving, the first line of defense is to do routine inspections and maintenance checks. By regularly inspecting the RV's tires, brakes, engine, and other essential components, owners can identify potential problems and take preventative measures to address them. In particular, tire care is necessary because blowouts can pose significant dangers to drivers and passengers. As part of their routine maintenance, RVers rotate their tires, check the pressure in their tires, and look for anything that might indicate wear. Understanding how the weight of the recreational vehicle is distributed and adhering to the load capabilities advised by the manufacturer are additional factors that contribute to the longevity of tires and overall road safety.

To ensure that the engine of their recreational vehicle (RV) continues to function smoothly, RV owners undertake routine checks on fluids such as oil, transmission fluid, and coolant. The RV's electrical system, including the batteries and wiring, should be inspected regularly to lower the risk of electrical breakdowns while the RV is on the road. Plumbing systems, another essential component of RV living, are subjected to routine inspections to ensure they are free of leaks, obstructions, and functioning issues. RVers have the opportunity to get more familiar with the complexities of their vehicles through routine inspections, which helps them develop a sense of self-reliance and confidence in their ability to address possible problems.

RV owners should be prepared for the possibility of experiencing failures and malfunctions, even if they do preventative maintenance, with the utmost diligence. They are resourceful and have a fundamental understanding of troubleshooting, which becomes a precious ability when addressing repairs while on the move. Many people who own recreational vehicles (RVs) provide themselves with toolkits that contain essential tools for performing basic maintenance. These tools include electrical testers, screwdrivers, and wrenches. Having the ability to recognize and fix fundamental problems, such as loose connections, minor leaks, or faulty fuses, allows RV owners to resolve difficulties and resume their travels quickly.

Both the interior and outside of the RV can be troubleshooted, and minor repairs can be performed. Awnings, slide-out mechanisms, and entry steps are examples of exterior parts that are susceptible to wear and may require changes or repairs in the future. During travel, interior components such as appliances, furnishings, and plumbing fixtures are easy to wear and tear if not properly maintained. RVers can keep their living space functioning and comfortable if they are skilled at locating the source of problems and possess the tools necessary to solve them.

There are situations in which the assistance of a professional is required, even though many RV owners can perform minor repairs on their own. A strategic solution would be to establish a network of dependable RV service providers along the travel route to handle more complex repairs. To ensure that assistance is easily accessible whenever required, many RVers research and prepare lists of trustworthy repair shops and service facilities in various regions. RVers have a safety net in the form of the option to contact educated specialists who specialize in RV repairs. These professionals offer expertise and solutions beyond what can be accomplished through do-it-yourself efforts.

The RV's appliances and systems demand attention and maintenance, as well as the mechanical and structural factors that must be considered. The convenience and functionality of the recreational vehicle (RV) are directly correlated to the presence of kitchen appliances, heating and cooling systems, water heaters, and sanitary facilities. In order to guarantee the dependability and lifespan of these systems, it is essential to perform routine maintenance and cleaning and follow the instructions provided by the manufacturer. Taking preventative steps, such as checking propane systems for leaks and making sure there is adequate ventilation, helps to create a living environment that is both secure and effective within the recreational vehicle (RV).

It is not enough to have a comprehensive understanding of the RV itself to prepare for RV travel adequately; one must also ensure that required tools and spare parts are included in the preparation. By carrying a spare tire, fuses, light bulbs, and other widely used replacement parts, recreational vehicle owners can address problems in a timely manner without having to rely only on assistance from outside sources. Furthermore, access to user manuals, technical data, and internet resources is beneficial for troubleshooting and provides direction on repairs specific to the RV's make and model.

They can handle RV repairs while traveling, which presents several issues, including the unpredictability of breakdowns and the potential impact on travel plans. Recreational vehicle drivers have an adaptable mindset, as they know that unforeseen repairs may necessitate delays or alterations to the schedule. Embracing the unpredictability of living a nomadic lifestyle might serve as a method of coping with the pressures and uncertainties of traveling. Even though breakdowns might be annoying, they also present possibilities for unanticipated discoveries, unexpected relationships with local communities, and the creation of unforgettable stories that are essential to the RV experience.

Recreational vehicle (RV) owners frequently contribute to the community by sharing their experiences and thoughts, contributing to a collective knowledge base that benefits both seasoned travelers and those new to the lifestyle. Forums on the internet, groups on social media, and clubs for RV enthusiasts all serve as platforms where RV enthusiasts may share information, seek assistance, and discuss solutions to problems common to the hobby. Individuals in the RV community help one another through the ups and downs of life on the road, which contributes to the development of a sense of camaraderie fostered by the RV community's collaborative nature. Within the RV community, a dynamic network of assistance is created due to shared wisdom and direct experiences, which provide valuable tools for diagnosing and handling repairs.

It is also necessary to have some level of financial preparedness to adapt to the obstacles of RV maintenance while on the move. A wise technique for RV owners is creating a budget that accounts for routine maintenance, unexpected repairs, and emergencies. Even though do-it-yourself repairs can be beneficial in terms of cost, there are occasions in which the assistance of a professional is required. RVers who have money reserves for such circumstances can address problems without experiencing undue financial hardship. Extended warranties and roadside assistance plans are two additional options that many RV owners choose to purchase. These options offer extra security and peace of mind while traveling.

Not only does repairing RVs while on the move involve solving mechanical difficulties, but it also requires adopting a mindset that is self-sufficient and can adapt to changing circumstances. People who live in RVs develop the ability to solve problems effectively as they learn to negotiate the complexities of their homes on wheels and respond to obstacles with toughness and originality. In addition to increasing general contentment with the RV lifestyle, the sense of accomplishment from effectively troubleshooting and resolving issues contributes to this satisfaction. Every repair presents the owner with a new learning opportunity, contributing to their growing knowledge and confidence in their ability to handle the problematic aspects of RV ownership.

To summarize, the ability to handle RV repairs and maintenance while on the move is an essential component of the nomadic lifestyle. This particular facet of the lifestyle calls for a proactive attitude, inventiveness, and a willingness to adapt. RV owners take on the role of travelers and do-it-yourself mechanics, allowing them to cultivate a profound awareness of their vehicles and develop the skills necessary to address frequent problems. Self-sufficiency in recreational vehicles (RVs) can be achieved through habits such as routine maintenance, regular inspections, and having a toolkit that is adequately stocked. Developing relationships with service providers who are recognized as professionals

In addition, the ability to navigate repairs while on the road is further enhanced by tapping into the collective expertise of the RV community. One must maintain a flexible mindset, be financially prepared, and acknowledge that each repair contributes to the overall richness of the RV adventure to successfully navigate the problems that arise from unanticipated failures. Ultimately, the capability to handle repairs while on the go transforms RV ownership into an exciting and powerful adventure. This is because every difficulty becomes a chance for personal development, education, and the unending chase of the open road.

Staying Safe and Healthy During the Journey

Embarking on the open road in an RV is a liberating and transformative experience, offering unparalleled freedom and a connection with the diverse landscapes of the journey. Even in the middle of the adventure that is discovery, RV travelers' safety is still the most critical factor. Maintaining your health and safety while traveling is essential for the success of your RV experience as a whole and for enjoying the nomadic lifestyle. This essay explores the many facets of traveling safely and healthily, looking at the difficulties of living a nomadic lifestyle, the value of preventative measures, and incorporating wellness practices into the design of recreational vehicles.

RV travelers frequently find themselves in various climates and environments, which presents several fundamental issues. The range of landforms experienced, from the humid woods of the Southeast to the arid deserts of the Southwest, carries different weather patterns and possible health concerns. To adjust to these changes, one must be proactive in maintaining one's comfort and health and have a thorough understanding of how the environment affects the body. RVers frequently ensure they are dressed appropriately for the weather so they can travel through sweltering heat and freezing nights. Furthermore, staying hydrated becomes essential to overall health since tourists realize dehydration is more likely to occur in arid areas and take precautions to rehydrate frequently.

Proactive health measures cover RV travelers' lifestyles, not just climate-related factors. Long-distance driving is passive, which can have adverse health effects on the body, including cardiovascular problems and muscular stiffness. Because they understand exercise is important, RVers include regular workouts into their mobile lifestyle. Incorporating daily activities becomes essential, whether hiking in national parks, biking on beautiful paths, or doing yoga at a campsite. Walking over various landscapes in an RV creates a unique opportunity to connect with nature and improves mental and physical health.

Another essential component of health, nutrition, has its own set of difficulties when traveling in an RV. Meal preparation may be hampered by an RV's tiny kitchen and storage space, and there may be a strong temptation to rely on convenience meals. Nonetheless, a lot of RVers place a high priority on eating a balanced diet because they understand the close relationship between health and wellbeing. A balanced and nutritious diet when traveling can be achieved by preparing meals ahead of time, stocking up on fresh vegetables, and combining a range of food categories. Taking advantage of regional cuisines and local farmers' markets offers a gastronomic experience and promotes well-being by providing various fresh food options.

In the rush of travel, sleep is sometimes forgotten. Yet, it's essential for preserving health and safety. Achieving peaceful sleep can be difficult for RVers for various reasons, such as getting used to new surroundings, possible noise at campgrounds, and restricted sleeping options inside the RV. RV travelers must prioritize good sleep hygiene by setting up a cozy resting environment, following regular sleep routines, and engaging in relaxing activities before bed. RVers can create an ideal sleeping environment using blackout curtains, comfortable bedding, and ambient noise makers. This way, they can wake up feeling rejuvenated and prepared for the day's activities.

Sustaining one's mental wellbeing is just as important when living an RV lifestyle. The unpredictable nature of the road, the frequent change of scenery, and the possibility of solitude on long trips can all hurt one's mental health. RVers develop mental health care practices because they understand the value of self-care and balance. Taking up artistic endeavors like writing, photography, or other hobbies allows one to express themselves and unwind. Connecting with other RV enthusiasts at events, groups, or online reduces loneliness and promotes a sense of community. In addition, adopting mindfulness exercises like meditation or walks in the outdoors encourages resilience and mental clarity in the face of the difficulties that come with living a nomadic lifestyle.

Although freedom and flexibility are the hallmarks of most RV travel, several safety issues require close attention. As was covered in the previous essay, proper vehicle maintenance is essential to road safety. Frequent maintenance, pre-trip inspections, and timely resolution of mechanical concerns all enhance the RV's dependability and roadworthiness. The tires are critical to the safety of RV travel, so RVers prioritize prompt replacement, good inflation, and rotation to minimize blowouts and guarantee maximum traction.

When driving on new roads, inclement weather, and varied terrain, one must pay extra attention to road safety. RV drivers follow safe driving guidelines, which include observing speed limits, obeying traffic laws, and putting away electronic devices when driving. Many RV owners also spend money on safety measures like tire pressure monitoring systems and backup cameras to increase their awareness while driving. RVers can better plan their trips and make wise decisions to guarantee safety when they know road conditions, weather forecasts, and possible hazards.

Being ready for emergencies is essential to traveling in an RV safely. RVers prepare for emergencies by stocking emergency kits with necessary materials like tools, first aid supplies, and emergency communication equipment. Knowing how to use safety devices like fire extinguishers and emergency exits becomes crucial. RV drivers should know where emergency services are located along their trip and should always have contact information for towing and roadside help. Maintaining composure in the face of unforeseen circumstances aids in successful problem-solving and guarantees the safety of drivers and other road users.

Another factor that RVers consider to preserve a safe and pleasurable travel experience is campground safety. Selecting respectable campgrounds guarantees a degree of safety and facilities that enhance general well-being, whether private or public. RVers frequently recommend and review campgrounds to one another within the community, generating.

It is an essential resource for people looking for cozy

and secure lodging. Everyone who camps in the area benefits from a courteous and safe atmosphere when they know the restrictions, including quiet hours and security procedures.

Healthcare concerns are crucial to ensure well-being

when traveling in an RV. Because they understand how important it is to be close to healthcare services, RVers frequently plan their trips with access to medical facilities in mind. Carrying first aid supplies, prescription drugs, and medical records has become commonplace. To provide even more security and peace of mind, many RVers also get medical emergency travel insurance. When telehealth services are incorporated into the nomadic lifestyle, recreational vehicle owners can obtain medical consultations from a distance and care for their non-emergency healthcare needs while traveling.

For RVers, water safety is a top priority, mainly when

using external water sources or campsite amenities. RV travelers' general health is enhanced by taking proactive steps to ensure the safety and quality of drinking water. To ease worries about their water quality, some RVers purchase water filtration devices or bring bottled water with them. Water safety is further enhanced by following proper sanitary procedures within the RV, such as routinely cleaning the plumbing and tank systems.

The mobile lifestyle naturally involves embracing a

feeling of community and watching out for fellow RVers. RVers frequently exchange safety advice, travel ideas, and emergency contact details within the group, fostering a cooperative and encouraging network. With seasoned travelers helping newcomers to the lifestyle, the combined knowledge and experiences of the RV community are an excellent resource for remaining safe and healthy while traveling.

To sum up, maintaining one's health and safety while traveling is a complex process that considers one's physical and mental health, the safety of the vehicle, and emergency readiness. RVers take a proactive approach to safety, integrating precautions into their way of life to deal with the difficulties presented by various temperatures, shifting landscapes, and unpredictabilities on the road. RVers emphasize physical activity, a healthy diet, restful sleep, and mental health while balancing self-care and adventure. To enable RVers to travel freely and thoroughly enjoy their adventure, vehicle safety and emergency readiness become essential elements of the nomadic lifestyle. The collective wellbeing of travelers is improved when the RV community embraces a spirit of community and cooperation, forming a support system that goes beyond the road. Keeping oneself safe and healthy becomes a fundamental value that emphasizes the fulfillment and durability of the nomadic lifestyle in recreational vehicle travel, where the trip holds equal significance as the destination.

CONCLUSION

In the pages of "Roaming Retreat: RV Camping Bliss in America's National Treasures," readers embark on an immersive journey into the heart of the nomadic lifestyle, discovering the myriad wonders that await those who choose to roam the open road in the comfort of their RVs. This e-book is a thorough guide that combines the usefulness of recreational vehicle travel with the captivating charm of America's National Treasures. The electronic book provides a road plan for a journey that will always be remembered, from choosing the ideal recreational vehicle to creating a detailed schedule among the nation's most famous scenery.

The investigation starts with thoroughly examining RV travel, debunking popular myths such as [the notion that RV travel is only for retirees or the misconception that it's an expensive way to travel], and highlighting the many advantages of selecting this special mode of transportation for enjoying nature. Readers will gain knowledge on route planning, necessary equipment and supplies, and effective RV setup techniques as they progress through the chapters, guaranteeing a smooth and pleasurable camping experience. The e-book delves deeper into the intricate fabric of the United States' National Parks, illuminating not just the well-known sites but also the lesser-known treasures scattered throughout the terrain.

Beyond the usefulness, the e-book explores the essence of the RV lifestyle, including the friendships made while traveling, the relationships with the natural world, and the delight of sampling local foods and marketplaces. From seeing animals to making the most of outdoor living areas, the e-book captures the spirit of RV camping. It provides both first-time and experienced travelers with a plethora of knowledge and ideas.

Upon reaching the last chapters, the e-book skillfully focuses on the significance of road safety, well-being, and emergency preparedness. It highlights the importance of maintaining awareness while welcoming spontaneity and striking a balance between the excitement of discovery and responsible travel methods.

"Roaming Retreat" is essentially more than just a guidebook; it's a tribute to the allure of the wide road, a celebration of the nomadic spirit, and evidence of the transformational potential of RV camping in America's National Treasures. This e-book captures the essence of a Roaming Retreat—an adventure that transcends the ordinary, immerses in nature's wonders, and invites everyone to savor the bliss of RV camping in America's most treasured landscapes—whether one is an aspiring RVer looking for practical advice or an experienced enthusiast seeking new insights.

Thank you for buying and reading/ listening to our book. If you found this book useful/ helpful please take a few minutes and leave a review on the platform where you purchased our book. Your feedback matters greatly to us.